Winged Words from God

a collection of inspirational poems

Blessings,
Madeleine Beter

Winged Words from God

a collection of inspirational poems

Madeline Beber

WORD ASSOCIATION PUBLISHERS
www.wordassociation.com
1.800.827.7903

All Scripture references taken from the New International Version of the Bible

Copyright © 2014 by Madeline Beber
All rights reserved. No part of this book may be used or reproduced in any manner whatsoever without written permission of the author.
Printed in the United States of America.

ISBN: 978-1-63385-023-1

Library of Congress Control Number: 2014917863

Designed and published by
Word Association Publishers
205 Fifth Avenue
Tarentum, Pennsylvania 15084

www.wordassociation.com

1.800.827.7903

Dedicated
To
Our Wondrous Gracious God
Who reigns supreme
Lord of All
And
In Memory of
My Husband
Ron

Table of Contents

Prologue 11

Chapter 1 – God's Glory 15
    Preface 16
    A Glimpse of His Glory 17
    Golden Light 20
    -Our Gaze- 22
    -Regalia- 24
    High Flying Clouds 27
    A Momentous Moment 30
    Bejeweled 33
    Spectacular Display 36
    The View 39
    Before the Throne 41
    Within the Misty Light 44
    Glory Road 46
    Supremely Stunning 49

Chapter 2 – God's Sovereignty and Justice 53
    Preface 54
    By God's Orchestration 55
    Hope Springs Eternal 57
    WHY? 59
    Timeless Change 62
    From This Height 65
    Night Sounds 68
    "Justice" 71
    By God's Appointment 74
    In the Map room of the Almighty 77

Chapter 3 – God's Grace 81
    Preface 82
    -Alive- 83
    -CLEAN- 86

Out of Darkness 89
RUBY RED 92
"Monopoly" Grace 95
White as Snow 98
Still Alive 101
Behind the Veil 104
Morning Grace 107
Eclipse 110
Unchanging Grace 113
Mud Puddle 116
Out of the Shadow 119
God's Dusting 122
"People Watching" 124
Glorious Liberty 127
Got Sludge? 130
"Flying High" 133
Clutter Clean-Up 136

Chapter 4 – God's Love 139
Preface 140
A Father's Love 141
Lasting Love 144
A Strand of Pearls 147
Ice Cream with K.J. 149
God's Promises 151
The Perfect Pumpkin 154
DISCIPLINED 157
Summer Rain 160
Enveloped in Love 162
Two Pink Roses 164
Beyond "ken"! 166
In Loving Closeness 169
Love's Kiss 172

Chapter 5 - God's Creation 175
Preface 176
DUSK 177
God in the Details 179

Unfettered Worship	181
The Life of the Tree	183
Mountaintop Calm	186
Nature's Praise	188
Life's Simple Pleasures	190

Chapter 6- God's Presence 193
Preface	194
Encircled	195
The Search	198
In the Wind	201
Out of the Fog	204
Snow's Dusting	206
Quiet Splendor	209
Ubiquity	212
Vanishing	215
Butterfly Bliss	218
-Distractions-	221
Above the Clouds	224
Dance of the Butterfly	227
Foggy Days	230

Chapter 7 - God's Power 233
Preface	234
A Mighty Wind	235
Beyond Greatness	238
-Mockingbird Taunt-	240
Above the Fray	243
The Battle	247
The Mighty Oak	249
The Rock	254

Chapter 8 - God's Wondrous Care and Enabling Hand .. 255
Preface	256
Wondrous Care	257
At Rope's End	260
Blanketed	263
Bear Care	266

Illuminated by God's Light 269
Restoration 271
The Small Stuff 274
"Look Up" 277
Dormant Trees 280
Perfection's Best 283
-Weeping Willow Waters- 286
Sliver Moon 288
The Misty Lowlands 290
The View from the Boat 293

Chapter 9- God's Call to the Believer 297
Preface 298
Almost Missed 299
Circles of Raindrops 302
Earnestly Seeking 305
Reflections 308
Living, well-watered 311
By the Wayside 314
Dancing in Midair 317
Death to the Palm 320
In God's Lane 323
Melodious Song 326
The Rut 329
Perspectives 332
Mirror Image 335
Orange Delight 338
The Journey 341
Poppies Unfurled 344
Hanging Out 346
Wasteland 349
-Pure Joy- 352
Reflection 355
"jump" 358
Summer Storm 361
"Busy as Bees" 364
THE TOUCH! 367
The Wait 370

Prologue

Have you ever felt God's hand upon your life? Has He ever set you aside for a time to accomplish something that you didn't quite understanding and at the onset, you were hesitant to even do it? You didn't understand the reason for it all and the purpose that He had in mind? You were even unsure of the future? You had no idea what the outcome would be in the end?

Let me tell you a story! It started long before I was born but I will not go into all the details of my entire life even though I know without a doubt that God is in control of every aspect of our lives even before we are born. But coming forward to the immediate present, this book started several years ago when God told me in His Word to not do something that I had been doing for many years, 25 years in fact. I had been a leader in a Bible Study Fellowship class for some time and God decided that I should not do that for a period of time in order to "write a book". Now if you had never written much of anything before, you would certainly think that would be a strange thing to do. And believe me, I asked Him. Are you sure? And His answer came in Genesis 12 where God called Abram to leave his country, his people and his father's household and go to the land that He would show him. I was so convinced of God's call upon my life that I withdrew from Bible Study Fellowship for a time…to write a book.

To many people, that would seem nonsensical and irrational, but I was fully convinced of God's call and enablement for me to do a task that I had no idea how I was going to accomplish. And so I began! Mind you, the book that I began to write, which is still incomplete, is not the book that God wrote! HIS book is a collection of His words over a period of time which came by His design, not mine.

So I began "my" book and in the midst of writing, tragedy hit! My husband of 44 years became very sick. The onset of pancreatic cancer took my beloved husband, Ron, in a matter of two months. It was so quick and he was gone; taken by the hand of God but all according to His plan and purpose. In order for me to say that, you must understand that the road that God lays out before you is never easy and sometimes is filled with hardship and great pain. God, however, is our great Comforter and Provider in and through the storm.

I remember one specific day as I was in the midst of going back and forth from home to the rehabilitation center where my husband was after a stroke that he had had; God met me in my heartache and tears along the drive home with a glorious sunset amongst gorgeous clouds aglow with the setting sun; rays of light shining forth in all directions creating a shimmering lining behind the clouds and an awesome awareness of His presence and love for me and also an assurance of His care.

And so the poems began! "Beneath God's Wings" was the first of many written and each one along the way added to the collection. At first, they were therapy; a way to express the heartache that I felt after my husband passed away and with each month and day, the poems helped me to cope with the aloneness and loss that I felt.

I never intended on writing so many but God kept on sending them my way. As I tackled the garden which my husband had so lovingly cared for, God spoke to me through nature and His creation. The garden became a wellspring of hope and joy albeit a challenge to keep up and maintain. And the poems kept coming. At every turn, I saw God in a new and beautiful way and the words flew upon the page. I began to share each poem with others and they were changing people's lives in ways that only God could do. So I continued to write and before I knew it…I had indeed written a book, just as God had said that I would. Amazing!

Does God have a purpose and a plan for each person's life? Most decidedly so! His plan is perfect and all we have to do is obey when He calls. Do we always know the outcome? Most times not but we can trust Him, for…we know that in all things God works for the good of those who love him, who have been called according to his purpose (Romans 8:28). Does that mean that everything is going to be rosy and wonderful? By no means! But God is with us and for us in the midst of the challenge. Would I prefer to have my husband with me? Of course, but I look back and if God had not taken him in the manner and as quickly as He did, not **one** poem would have been written. God is sovereign! His "Will" will be done! Our lives are changed as we step out in faith to follow the path that God has put before us. I'm sure that Abraham had no idea that God would indeed make him the father of the nation of Israel.

And so…it is with gratefulness and thanksgiving that I lay before you the poems that the Lord has so graciously given to me. May they touch your heart and change your life in order that you will follow more closely to our glorious Savior who is Lord of all. These poems are indeed "Winged Words from God".

Beneath God's Wings

In the shadow of God's wings,
    Is our shelter from the storm!
There's a place of total safety,
    A refuge from all harm!

In the shadow of God's wings,
    There's faithfulness we can know.
A place of complete security,
    His care and love to show.

In the shadow of God's wings
    Rests His comfort and His care,
To see us through the trials of life,

His confidence to share!

In the shadow of God's wings,
    Are many saints, our load to bear,
Providing for our every need,
    Showing us they truly care.

In the shadow of God's wings,
    We are kept within His hand,
To witness to all those around,
    Where deliverance is found!

In the shadow of God's wings,
    Salvation rests secure,
Our peace and joy and fruitfulness,
    Our trust in Christ is sure.

In the shadow of God's wings,
    We truly know we're loved,
We are ever in His presence,
    He gives us His joy from up above.

In the shadow of God's wings,
    We can truly be at rest,
For within His gentle loving grasp,
    We really have God's very best.

Scriptures:

- Psalm 16 All – v.11- …you will fill me with joy in your presence,…
- Psalm 17:8 – Keep me as the apple of your eye; hide me in the shadow of your wings.
- Psalm 91 All – v.4- He will cover you with his feathers, and under his wings you will find refuge; his faithfulness will be your shield and rampart.

God's deliverance through trying times!

Chapter 1
God's Glory

Psalm 19:1 – The heavens declare the glory of God; the skies proclaim the work of his hands

Hebrews 1:3 – The Son is the radiance of God's glory and the exact representation of his being, sustaining all things by his powerful word.

Preface

Do we truly know what God's glory is like? Can we see it with our two eyes or feel and touch it with our hands? God's complete glory is unknowable and untouchable to mankind. It is completely other than us and our sphere of living. It is far beyond our understanding, seemingly out of our grasp in this life. And yet…God makes Himself known to us in many ways on various levels and areas of our lives. We are allowed "a glimpse" into the supremely glorious God who reigns sovereign over all things from before the beginning of time itself.

Have you ever desired to get a glimpse of God's glory? Moses desired to see God's glory face to face (Genesis 33:12-23). He asked God to show him His glory and God said, "I will cause all my goodness to pass in front of you, and I will proclaim my name, the LORD, in your presence. …But…you cannot see my face, for no one may see me and live." And God's glory passed by the cleft in the rock where Moses stood while Moses was covered by the hand of God. Moses saw only God's back, but how awesome that would be. Even to see a part of God's glory would be so far beyond what we could take in. What a privilege Moses was given to see God even in part.

However, we are also privileged to have a view of God's glory that Moses never had. We have God's Holy Word, the Bible, given to us in order that we might see God's glory within the pages. God does indeed proclaim His name and who He is among the folds of His Word. And God does pass in front of us His goodness in the creation He has made. How can you not see Him in the very nature He created by His own hand and word. If you truly desire to see God's glory, look to the heavens, the sky, the trees and the birds of the field. You will see God's handiwork amid His creation and marvel at the Creator and His glory and praise His holy name!

But remember…it is only a glimpse of God's glory! God is so far beyond our imagining or understanding. God is glorious in all His ways. To God be the glory, forever and ever!

A Glimpse of His Glory

The orchid tree is in bloom across the way
A profusion of translucent delicate pink blossoms
Weighing down the branches
Brilliant, glorious, mildly fragrant
Bringing an abundance of bees humming round about
Casting forth a carpet of blooms beneath the tree
Like pink snow upon the ground, unbridled in splendor
"A glimpse" of a wondrous Creator!
Likewise a glorious sunrise at the break of day
Vibrant in radiant colors of vermillion, pinks and oranges
Aglow, filling the sky from horizon to horizon
"A glimpse" of God's radiant Light!

Or perhaps a mountain rising high
Majestic, strong in solid granite, immovable
Supremely beautiful in the morning sunshine
"A glimpse" of God's majesty and sovereign power!
All declaring His glory!
All giving "a glimpse" of who He is!
Take a look at the expanse of the ocean
Stretching from sky to sky
Reminding us of God's wondrous grace
A "glimpse" of how far God has removed our sin away
As far as the east is from the west
So many pictures into God's character
"A glimpse" into who God is!
Especially as we look into His Word, within the Bible's pages
A glimpse so profound, page upon page
Giving glimpses of our majestic Lord
Men who have gone before like Moses before the "burning bush"
Within the cleft of the rock glimpsing God as He walked by

Or Isaiah in the throne room of the Almighty
Overwhelmed by the LORD's presence
Also the disciples
Privileged witnesses of Christ's transfiguration
A glimpse into the beauty of Christ in their presence
Likewise Paul on the road to Damascus
Blinded by the dazzling light of Jesus
Changed by a glimpse of the Son of God
The book of Revelation was John's glimpse into the future
A "glimpse" of a God who is the Alpha and Omega
But the greatest picture of all!
The Cross of Christ
A glimpse of God's never ending love for His lost children
A glimpse of His amazing love for us!
For Christ died to save us from sin and death.
If you want to see the Father; take a glimpse at Jesus
He is the exact representation of God, the Almighty
Take a long glimpse; a glimpse of His extreme love for you!
A glimpse of His glory!

Scriptures:

- EXODUS 3 ALL - … "God said to Moses, "I AM WHO I AM."

- EXODUS 33:12-23 – Then Moses said, "Now show me your glory."…Then the LORD said, … "When my glory passes by, I will put you in the cleft in the rock and cover you with my hand until I have passed by.

- ISAIAH 6:1-5 - …I saw the LORD seated on a throne, high and exalted, and the train of his robe filled the temple. "Holy, holy, holy is the LORD Almighty; the whole earth is full of his glory."

- MATTHEW 17:1-8, MARK 9:2-8, LUKE 9:28-36 – Jesus'

transfiguration – There he (Jesus) was transfigured before them. His face shone like the sun, and his clothes became as white as the light.

- ACTS 9:1-19 - …As he (Saul) neared Damascus on his journey, suddenly a light from heaven flashed around him. "I am Jesus, whom you are persecuting,…

- HEBREWS 1 ALL – v.3 – The Son is the radiance of God's glory and the exact representation of his being, sustaining all things by his powerful word.

- I JOHN 4:10 – This is love: not that we loved God, but that he loved us and sent his Son as an atoning sacrifice for our sins.

- REVELATION 21:1-7 - … "I am the Alpha and the Omega, the Beginning and the End. … He who overcomes will inherit all this, and I will be his God and he will be my son."

Desiring to see His Glory!

Golden Light

Dawn
Early morning's glow
A mist lingers in the air
Daybreak's chill giving way to God's radiant sunrise
Warmth
Basking in the golden light
Filling every crevice of the earth
Penetrating rays falling on the distant landscape
Touching mountains in glorious beauty
Turning fluttering leaves to sparkling gems
Transforming even tree bark into a golden shimmer
Dew upon the grass turned to diamonds
The surface of ponds and lakes translucent in the glow
Changing ground and hills to a golden yellowy hue
The brilliant sun giving light in glittering array
Lighting upon our faces like a gentle kiss
Causing even the birds to take notice
In a cacophony of melodious song
Morning has begun
The day has taken flight
In God's golden light!
In His presence! His splendor and glory!

As our day begins
God reveals His presence
Making Himself known to all who seek Him
Those who care to see Him and desire to embrace Him as Lord
The Light of His Presence to the entire world
Giving light and life to all who believe
Filling us with His Holy Spirit
Touching every facet of our lives

Turning us into jewels in His crown
Giving purpose and meaning to our day
To an otherwise obscure life
Changing us from the inside out
Causing us to sing His praises
To worship and adore Him
God's glorious Presence
Jesus!
Emmanuel, God with us!
God's exact representation
The Light of the world!
Radiant and dazzling
Penetrating, piercing the darkness in our hearts
God's golden Light!
Glorious! Beyond description!
Aglow in splendor for all eternity!

Scriptures:

- GENESIS 1:3-5 – And God said, "Let there be light," and there was light.

- PSALM 76:4 – You are resplendent with light, more majestic than mountains rich with game.

- JOHN 1:4-9 – In him was life, and that life was the light of men.

- JOHN 8:12 - … "I am the light of the world. Whoever follows me will never walk in darkness, but will have the light of life."

- I JOHN 1:5-7 - …God is light; in him there is no darkness at all.

- REVELATION 22:5 – There will be no more night. They will not need the light of a lamp or the light of the sun, for the Lord God will give them light. And they will reign for ever and ever.

Basking in His light!

-Our Gaze-

Within our eye's view
To gaze upon God's beauty in the wonder of a flower;
    To gaze upon a mountain, tall in majesty and power
To gaze and see the gusting wind rustling through the trees;
    To gaze upon drifting clouds, blowing where they please
To gaze upon a mother gnatcatcher skimming the lawn for bugs,
    To feed a baby hatchling with God's provision from above
To see a gentle sleeping child resting serene in peacefulness,
    Surrounded by God's protection and loving faithfulness.
All these wonders, we enjoy and rest within our gaze;
    God's blessings, His creation, His grandeur on display!

Our view askew
Perhaps your gaze is less than grand, filled with much despair;
    Many days of hardship, troubles and worldly cares
Perhaps you are surrounded by loneliness and four walls;
    Waiting for the phone to ring but no one cares to call.
Perhaps your home is filled with strife and daily harsh conflict;
    Or a spouse who is unfaithful, not the man you picked
Perhaps financial worries confront you each and every day;
    You see no sure end in sight; you cannot find your way.
Sometimes circumstances in our life really seem unfair;
    But there's One who is our refuge; we are in His care!

Our intentioned view
What is ever before you; what rests within your view?
    Oft-times things before our eyes are objects we pursue.
Our eyes can gaze on good or bad, the pure and not so holy;
    But available before our eyes is Jesus, the One and Only.
He's far beyond our earthly view but yet within our sight;
    He alone is faithful, filled with power, awesome might.

To gaze upon His gentle face, to know His peace and love;
> To see His worth and goodness, His blessings from above
To gaze upon His beauty as glorious King upon the throne;
> To worship and adore Him, the Living One forevermore!

Our future view

So let our gaze be fixed on Christ, the matchless One Supreme.
> How beautiful to seek His face, to Him our praises bring.
What glory shall assail our eyes in God's most heavenly place!
> To gaze upon the Lord of all and see Him face to face!

Scriptures:

- Psalm 27 All - …One thing I ask of the LORD, this is what I seek: …to gaze upon the beauty of the LORD…Your face, LORD, I will seek…I will see the goodness of the LORD in the land of the living.
- Psalm 119:18 - Open my eyes that I may see wonderful things in your law.
- Proverbs 4:20-27 - …fix your gaze directly before you.
- Isaiah 6:1-3 - …I saw the LORD seated on a throne, high and exalted,… "Holy, holy, holy is the LORD Almighty; the whole earth is full of his glory."
- Matthew 6:22-23 – The eye is the lamp of the body.
- Hebrews 12:2 – Let us fix our eyes on Jesus, the author and perfecter of our faith,…
- Revelation 1:12-18 – "…I am the First and the Last. I am the Living One; I was dead and behold I am alive for ever and ever!"…

Fixing my gaze upon Christ, the exalted One

-Regalia-

Clothed in nobility
Dressed in finery
Elegant and majestic
Crowned in fairest beauty
Blooming erect in magnificence
On straight sturdy stems
Stately, reaching skyward
Blowing and swaying gently in the breeze
The iris plant of the family Iridaceae
In Greek meaning rainbow
Royalty in bloom
Delicate velvety petals laced in deep purple splendor
Spreading out from a golden center
Glorious!
A flower of royal standing bedecked in graceful elegance
Decorated in royal robes of color
A symbol of kingly majesty
Regal character in nature's garden
The iris
Regalia on display!

Who is above all robed in majesty?
The One displayed in splendor
Magnificent in glory, crowned above all others
The One who stands victorious
Strong and supremely sovereign in all His ways
Reigning upon His heavenly throne
High and exalted
At the right hand of God ruling in righteousness
Governing the nations
In beauty for all to see

The train of His garments filling the temple
Glorious!
Lord of lords and King of kings!
Bedecked in holiness and purity, righteous in all His ways
Christ Jesus!
In regalia in the heavenly realms!

Are we not to be like Him?
A display of His majesty and splendor
Putting our trust in His saving grace
A witness of who He is
Are we not to be robed in His righteousness?
Christ-like in our character?
Following in His footsteps?
Growing in beauty and holiness?
Destined to reign with Him eternally
Recipients of a glorious inheritance
Forever and ever
Receiving a crown to gratefully lay at the feet Jesus
Our Mighty and Majestic King!
Christ Jesus!
Reigning in glorious regalia!

SCRIPTURES:

- PSALM 93 ALL – The LORD reigns, he is robed in majesty… armed with strength.

- ISAIAH 6:1-4 – I saw the LORD seated on a throne, high and exalted and the train of his robe filled the temple…

- II CORINTHIANS 3:18 – And we, who with unveiled faces all reflect the Lord's glory, are being transformed into his likeness with ever-increasing glory, which comes from the Lord, who is the Spirit.

- I Timothy 6:11-16 – God, the blessed and only Ruler, the King of kings and Lord of lords,…
- Revelation 1:12-16 – … "like a son of man,"… His face was like the sun shining in all its brilliance.
- Revelation 11:15 – … "The kingdom of the world has become the kingdom of our Lord and of his Christ, and he will reign for ever and ever."

To God be the glory!

High Flying Clouds

Look up!
Stretching out across earth's atmosphere
Paper thin
Elevated to the upper stratosphere
Cirrostratus clouds
Moving slowly above the distant ground below
Casting their shadow on the earth
In obscure patterns and shapes
Bringing cooling relief
Shade from the hot summer sun
But
Withholding much needed rain
Marching in waves across the sky
In precise order like a marching band
Floating suspended in midair
Puffy, billowy
Drifting on the wind
Spreading forth
Like finely woven lace
Dressed in purest white
Set against a brilliant blue background
God's wondrous creation!
Robed in majesty and wonder
Even clouds proclaim
His glory!

What do you see when clouds come into your life?
Dark clouds of uncertainty
Tragedy or sickness and pain
Stretching out before you
Moving into your every thought

Blanketing your days
Taking precedence over your life
Casting a shadow on your very existence
Withholding joy and happiness
How do you view those clouds of darkness?

Did you not know?
Those clouds of doubt and despair
Most certainly remain a part of our lives
In varying degrees
But
There is another view to behold
For clouds have a beauty all their own
"Sometimes" they are sent
By the hand of God
Causing us to look up!
Causing us to rest in the shadow of His love
Relying upon Him
Seeking Him for comfort and relief
From our despair and hopelessness
Helping us
To float on realms on high
To focus our eyes and thoughts on Him
Those clouds
Draw us to His very presence
Causing us to see Him more clearly
For in the midst of the clouds
There also can be
The glory of a sunset!

How will you view the clouds in your life?

Scriptures:

- Psalm 55:22 – Cast your cares on the LORD and he will sustain you, he will never let the righteous fall.
- Psalm 91 All – v.1 – He who dwells in the shelter of the Most High will rest in the shadow of the Almighty.
- Isaiah 40:25-31 - ...Lift your eyes and look to the heavens...The LORD is the everlasting God, the Creator of the ends of the earth.
- I Peter 5:6-11 - ...the God of all grace...will himself restore you and make you strong, firm and steadfast.
- Revelation 1:7 – Look, he is coming with the clouds, and every eye will see him, even those who pierced him; and all the peoples of the earth will mourn because of him. So shall it be! Amen.

Focusing on the Glory of God, not the clouds!

A Momentous Moment

Eyes aglow, opened wide
Peering into the old wooden box
The mystery, the fascination and wonder
Two little boys and their grandmother
Enjoying a cherished moment together
As each piece is carefully unwrapped
One by one selected out of the box
Revealing each figurine nesting within the tissue paper
Wow! Oohs and aahs!
The shepherds with their sheep
The wise men each bringing their gift
A cow! A donkey! Camels from afar!
Mary and Joseph
The angel of the Lord!
All positioned and arranged on top of the piano
Each gathered round
With one final addition
The little baby Jesus!
Two little boys in awe gazing in wonder and delight
Upon the manger scene
Upon the Lord of heaven and earth!
A momentous moment in time!

Can you imagine?
The wonder of it all! So long ago!
The shepherds looking with amazement upon the heavenly host
Leaving their sheep, to gaze upon the lowly manger scene
To view the glory of Jesus' birth
Imagine their reverential awe at the feet of their Savior and Lord
Wow! Can words express what took place there?
The silent night!

The calm and peace
A simple stable with ox and lamb nearby
The birthplace of the King of kings!
And when the wise men came, traveling from afar
Led by a glorious star
Bearing gifts with hearts to worship
Their reverent joy to gaze upon a gentle little child
The long awaited One!
The King foretold
A momentous moment in time!
So long ago!

But there is a time, a foretold moment coming
When we will gaze in reverent awe
Upon the One who died to save us all
Jesus Christ, our Risen Lord!
The splendor and the majesty
The awesome wonder when Christ returns again
When we shall all arise and meet Him in the air
To see Him face to face!
A momentous moment in glory!
Are you ready to meet your Lord, the Hope of Salvation?

Scriptures:

- Psalm 8 All – v.2a – From the lips of children and infants you have ordained praise…

- Isaiah 9:6-7 – For unto us a child is born, to us a son is given,…

- Matthew 1:19-2:12 – v.23 – "The virgin will be with child and will give birth to a son, and they will call him Immanuel"—which means, "God with us."

- Matthew 19:13-15, Mark 10:13-16, Luke 18:15-17 – Jesus said, "Let the little children come to me, and do not hinder them,

for the kingdom of heaven belongs to such as these."

- LUKE 2:1-20 – The Birth of Jesus/The Shepherds and the Angels – v.14 – "Glory to God in the highest, and on earth peace to men on whom his favor rests."
- I THESSALONIANS 4:13-18 - …For the Lord himself will come down from heaven…we who are still alive and are left will be caught up…to meet the Lord in the air. And so we will be with the Lord forever.

Giving thanks to God for every precious moment in life Waiting each day for Christ's return!

"Bejeweled"

A cold frost settled in, encapsulating the landscape
During the night-watches of the night
Super cold!
A startling crispness to the air
Crystal clear with a stark frigid chill
Bringing forth a pristine awakening to the day
In the morning light, everything was white!
Mountains covered in ice and misty clouds
Dressed in beauty and majesty
House rooftops painted with dazzling whiteness
Hiding shingles beneath a frosty coating
Icicles hanging from eaves like sparkling tinsel
Branches and trees bending low
Lawns changed to diamond studded carpets
In the first rays of sunshine
The tops of cars frosted with snowflake patterns
Windows fogged over in the cold morning air
The "bling" of winter!
The world decked out in finest garb with sparkle and glitter
God's Creation clothed in purest white!
Frosting! Bejeweled!

Oh, holy night with starry lights!
The sparkle and wonder of an earth changing event!
Christ's wondrous birth! Jesus bending low to earth!
Imagine!
As Mary and Joseph settled into that lowly stable
With stars shining brightly in the stillness of the night
With calmness and in peace
God's purpose and plan made clear
Bringing forth a newborn son

Son of God—Son of man!
The heavens declared the glory of His birth!
While shepherds tend their sheep in the fields
The heavenly host of angels declared the wondrous birth
Giving adoration and praise
With a radiant star shining brightly in the east
Its brilliance lighting the way in a clear night sky
With light never fading
Leading the Magi to worship the newborn King
The glory of the night of Christ's coming!
A world in stillness, peace and calm
For Emmanuel, God with us is born!
Pure and sinless arrayed in splendor and clothed in majesty
King of kings and Lord of lords! The One who reigns on high!
Oh, that we would come to worship and adore Him!
Remembering all that He has given to us
Life eternal, blessings in the heavenly realms
He has forgiven our sin and cleansed our hearts
Arrayed us in His robes of righteousness
Clothed us as children of the everlasting Father
Loved us with an everlasting love!
Bejeweled!

Scriptures:

- Psalm 19:1-6 – The heavens declare the glory of God; the skies proclaim the work of his hands.

- Psalm 30:11-12 – …you removed my sackcloth and clothed me with joy,…O LORD my God, I will give you thanks forever.

- Psalm 51:7-12 – …wash me, and I will be whiter than snow… Create in me a pure heart, O God, and renew a steadfast spirit within me,…

- Isaiah 61:10 – …For he has clothed me with garments of

salvation and arrayed me in a robe of righteousness,...as a bride adorns herself with her jewels.

- Matthew 2:1-12 - ...they went on their way, and the star they had seen in the east went ahead of them until it stopped over the place where the child was. When they saw the star, they were overjoyed.
- Luke 2:1-20 – The Birth of Jesus. ...Suddenly a great company of the heavenly host appeared with the angel, praising God and saying, "Glory to God in the highest, and on earth peace to men on whom his favor rests."
- Revelation 21 All – The New Jerusalem - ...the Holy City, Jerusalem, coming down out of heaven from God. It shone with the glory of God, and its brilliance was like that of a very precious jewel, like a jasper, clear as crystal. ...the glory of God gives it light, and the Lamb is its lamp.

May we come and worship Christ the LORD!

Supremely Stunning

Unbelievably stunning!
Stretching out across sky's expanse
God's spectacular ending to the day
A brilliant sunset in finest array
Ablaze in glowing shimmering colors
Vivid reds and gold melting into soft peach and purple
Vibrant! Beautiful!
Interspersed with fluffy clouds
Reflective of the sun's fading rays
Holding one's attention in quiet stillness
Leaving one speechless
Touching the senses
Directing our thoughts
Toward the Sovereign Creator of the universe
Pay attention! Take notice!
So quickly gone
Vanishing before your eyes
The passing of a supremely stunning event!

Time continues onward
Event after event
Day upon day
But there is "a day"
Quickly approaching, like a thief in the night
A day like no other
The day of the Lord!
Supremely stunning in its coming!
The Lord, Christ Jesus
Our Redeemer, Savior and King
Coming in the clouds in splendor and majesty
Riding on the wind

Glorious, holy and righteous
Beautiful beyond explaining
Leaving one speechless
Bringing our thoughts and hearts and minds
To the One who is worthy
Pay attention! Take notice!
He comes!
The Bridegroom cometh for His bride
To gather His children unto Himself
Those who love and believe in Him
In the blink of an eye
We shall be caught up with Him in the air
To rule and to reign
To come into His presence
Meeting Him face to face
To abide with Him forever
In wonder and thankful praise
Don't be left behind!
The day quickly approaches
Are you ready?
Prepared for this supremely stunning event!
Dear Jesus! Please come quickly!

SCRIPTURES:

- JOEL 2:10-14 – The day of the LORD is great; it is dreadful. Who can endure it.

- MATTHEW 24:1 – 25:13 – Therefore keep watch, because you do not know the day or the hour.

- JOHN 14:1-4 – And if I go and prepare a place for you, I will come back and take you to be with me that you also may be where I am.

- II Corinthians 5:1-10 – Our heavenly dwelling
- I Thessalonians 4:13-18 – The Coming of the Lord
- II Peter 3:1-13 – The Day of the Lord
- Revelation 16:15 – "Behold, I come like a thief! Blessed is he who stays awake and keeps his clothes with him,…
- Revelation 19:1-18 – 'Blessed are those who are invited to the wedding supper of the Lamb!'"

Watching! Excited for the Lord's return

— The View —

The panoramic view is breath-taking and spectacular
At the very crest of the mountain
Stretching out all around in every direction
To meet the earth's distant and curved horizon
At this high elevation, the long trek upward
Was rather winding and arduous
But without a doubt, well worth it all
To see a vista so majestic and glorious

Even in the middle of the long days of summer,
There are still patches of snow to be found;
Amongst the large rocks and boulders
Strewn about on the rocky ground
The cold air rustles in the forest pines below;
A crispy fresh breeze turning your cheeks aglow
Finding a lone rock to sit in stillness and gaze;
The glory of the view; how can you not be amazed!

However marvelous and oh so awesome
This mountain view before our eyes;
There is a higher, grander view
Beyond what we see and can realize.
Reigning in all His grace and glory;
Sovereign in everything He does;
God Almighty rules in splendor,
Our Holy King upon His heavenly throne!

Nothing compares to His glory
His majesty rules supreme;
His power is beyond imagining
And yet He cares for me

His wisdom is far from our understanding;
He's the everlasting God.
He gives strength unto the weary
As we rely upon His Word.

So, even though the mountains soar all around our feet
And God's striking beauty surrounds us everywhere;
May we see the Lord above with a grand and higher view?
An exalted One to worship, praise and always pursue
For though God is true and holy
And high and lifted up
He is always faithful and cares for His children;
For He loves us oh so very much!

Scripture:

- PSALM 8:1-9 – O LORD, our LORD, how majestic is your name in all the earth!

- PSALM 29:2-4,7-11 - …worship the LORD in the splendor of his holiness.

- PSALM 108:1-5 – For great is your love, higher than the heavens; your faithfulness reaches to the skies.

- ISAIAH 40:21-31 - "To whom will you compare me? Or who is my equal?" says the Holy One.

Awed by the view of God and His beauty!

Before the Throne!

Take notice!
The hummingbird feeder is empty!
Oh, dear! What shall we do?
But that someone would so graciously tend and fill it, please!
What sweet nectar!
Ambrosia to hungry thirsting hummingbirds
They flock around in vibrating clusters
Buzzing each other for position, a place at the feeder
Guzzling and taking in the delightful mixture
Dancing with delight, zipping round about, up and down
All beautifully dressed and wondrous to behold
Iridescent emerald green and vibrant ruby-throated red
Startling brilliant colors
And yet…one above all the rest in splendor and glory
Golden, russet plumage glistening forth
Glowing bright in shimmering light
Tail feathers marked with copper, black and white
The Rufous hummingbird of the northwest
Migrating southwardly; a rare sight
Momentarily making his home in the spacious backyard
Gathering round the plentiful feeder with all the others
How glorious!
Oh, that we would have the same characteristics!
Desiring to be fed, thirsting for more of God
Seeking to be filled to overflowing by the precious Word of God
Desiring to intimately know God and His indwelling Holy Spirit
To gather in fellowship with other believers
Coming together in worship and praise
Before the throne of our Lord!

What a beautiful picture!

Can you imagine?
When we enter into His rest, when the final trumpet sounds
When God calls His children home
To reside with Him forevermore
All the saints and believers assembled and gathered round
Before the throne of God beneath the canopy of heavenly glory
In the presence of the Holy One
Christ Jesus, our Lord!
For He is the splendid One!
Dressed in royal robes of righteousness
Glowing bright in shimmering light
Beautiful and Worthy of all our praise
Yet marked with the scars of His sacrifice
A reminder of His great love for us
Reigning on High at the right hand of God Almighty
Everlasting King of kings and Lord of lords!
Inviting us to come!
To the wedding banquet of the Lamb of God
To worship and adore Him! Before the Throne!
Will you be there?

SCRIPTURES:

- I CHRONICLES 16:23-36 - …For great is the LORD and most worthy of praise;…

- PSALM 107:5-9 - …Let us give thanks to the LORD for his unfailing love…for he satisfies the thirsty and fills the hungry with good things.

- JOHN 7:37-39 - … "If anyone is thirsty, let him come to me and drink. Whoever believes in me, as the Scripture has said, streams of living water will flow from within him."

- HEBREWS 1 ALL - …The Son is the radiance of God's glory and the exact representation of his being, sustaining all things by his powerful word.

- HEBREWS 4:14-16 - …Let us then approach the throne of grace with confidence, so that we may receive mercy and find grace to help us in our time of need.
- I JOHN 4:13-21 - We know that we live in him and he in us, because he has given us of his Spirit. …We love because he first loved us.
- REVELATION 4 ALL - …there before me was a throne in heaven with someone sitting on it. …They lay their crowns before the throne and say: "You are worthy, our Lord and God, to receive glory and honor and power,…"
- REVELATION 22:1-5 - …There will be no more night. They will not need the light of a lamp or the light of the sun, for the Lord God will give them light. And they will reign for ever and ever.

Waiting expectantly to gather round the throne of Christ!

Within the Misty Light

The day started sunny
The sky crystal clear and bright
Not a cloud on the horizon
But gradually there was a subtle change coming
High overhead in the expansive atmosphere
A wispy cast enveloping the blue sky
Not clouds per say, but a radiant misty haze
Only enough to diminish the sun's rays
Filtering the dazzling light of day
Causing the sky to turn to gentle softness
A golden glow!
Changing the landscape
Illuminating everything within a calming aura
A warmth of delicate light
Penetrating, piercing, yet gently cradling
Like being wrapped in a loving embrace
A hug from God's creation!
God's wondrous light!
Shining earthward
Oh, to remain here forever!
Within the misty light!
Within God's loving embrace
Oh, that we would desire to stay
Cradled in His loving arms
Never to leave
For He is the Light of the world
Penetrating our hearts
Transforming us into a new creation
Causing us to walk in newness of life
Changing the harshness of this world
Into realms of glory!

Allowing us to see the beauty that surrounds us
Causing us to find rest in Him
To learn and grow in His love
Hearing the softness of His whispering Holy Spirit
Gently leading us
Down pleasant pathways, along quiet waters
Oh, that we would seek to follow Him!
To remain within His embrace
There to experience love and joy and peace forevermore!
Within the misty light!

SCRIPTURES:

- ISAIAH 60:1-3, 19-22 – "Arise, shine, for your light has come, and the glory of the Lord rises upon you. …The sun will no more be your light by day, nor will the brightness of the moon shine on you, for the LORD will be your everlasting light, and your God will be your glory."

- JOHN 8:12 – When Jesus spoke again to the people, he said, "I am the light of the world. Whoever follows me will never walk in darkness, but will have the light of life."

- HEBREWS 1:3 – The Son is the radiance of God's glory and the exact representation of his being, sustaining all things by his powerful word.

- I JOHN 1 ALL - …if we walk in the light, as he is in the light, we have fellowship with one another and the blood of Jesus, his Son, purifies us from all sin.

Desiring to stay within the Light of Christ and His Word

Glory Road

Early morning traffic, cars all hurrying to work
Businessmen, teachers, factory workers
Children on their way to school
Buses and trucks, cars turning, right and left
Semi trucks on their way to distant destinations
Traffic, hustle and bustle
The road stretching out ahead
Another day begins with fog and overcast skies
A dark beginning to the morning
Driving onward and up ahead a faint glow
Golden in the misty fog
Reflective light, getting brighter, closer
Glowing with greater intensity, the clouds and fog departing
Opening wide to brilliant blue sky
Surrounded by sunshine, giving warmth
Inviting, for up ahead is welcomed passage
An open road filled with God's glorious light
A glory road!

Are you on the Glory road? The ordained path of God?
Are you headed in the right direction?
Following His guidance, seeking His love?
Listening to the Holy Spirit's leading
Going where He wants you to go?
Or have you been misled going completely astray?
Not knowing which way to turn
Overwhelmed by the hazy world around you?
The hustle and bustle of life, the hurry and frustration
Turmoil and daily strife with disappointments and difficulties
Financial woes or health concerns
Oft-times hardships and failures hindering your way

Life's road is filled daily with many things.
But there is a road that never ends
Leading straight unhindered to God Himself
That road is stretched out before you
Don't despair, take heart; it's ever near
The glory road to heaven
A way planned by the Father's hand!
Through Christ, our Glorious Savior and Lord!
He is our pathway to God's Promised Land.
The One who has redeemed us and leads us onward
The road may be hard and rocky but Christ has gone before us.
He's paved the way with His precious saving blood
Giving us salvation and eternal life
Our path to God's peace and love

So don't delay! Hop on board that Glory road!
It's open up ahead to meet the Savior face to face!
In a city paved with streets of gold
To be with Christ forever, to live eternally!
Arriving at our destination on that glorious reunion day!
Welcomed in on God's heavenly Glory road!

SCRIPTURES:

- ISAIAH 40:3-5 – …prepare the way for the LORD;…a highway for our God.
- ISAIAH 54:10-13 – …yet my unfailing love for you will not be shaken.
- MATTHEW 7:13-14 – …narrow (is) the road that leads to life, and only a few find it.
- JOHN 3:16 – For God so loved the world that he gave his one and only Son, that whosoever believes in him shall not perish but have eternal life.

- I Peter 5:10-11 – And the God of all grace, who called you to his eternal glory in Christ, after you have suffered a little while, will himself restore you and make you strong, firm and steadfast. To him be the power forever and ever. Amen.
- II Peter 1:3-11 - …and you will receive a rich welcome into the eternal kingdom of our Lord and Savior Jesus Christ.
- Revelation 21 and 22 All – v. 21:21 - …The great street of the city was of pure gold, like transparent glass…

On God's Glory road!

Spectacular Display

Summertime
The baseball game is over
The glaring stadium lights are quenched
Darkness fills the sky
There is a hush of quiet anticipation
Instantly the air comes alive in fireworks glory
Rockets soar on high bursting into life
Rising ever higher in brilliant splendor
Flashes of light and sparkle
Shooting stars and glittery circles
Exploding in shimmering pizzazz
Arrayed in vivid colors
Violet, orange and green
Crackling with shining stars
Streamers and dazzling red hearts
Booming into the atmosphere
Blazing before your eyes
Red, white and blue
A glorious banner of patriotism
Blasts of fiery sparks skirting across the skyline
Thundering loudly with pounding percussion
Taking your breath away
Nighttime's spectacular display!

Can such a spectacle be outdone?
In all its glory and glitz?
Undoubtedly!
Beyond the wonder of a fireworks display…
There is One who rises above
Who outshines all that this world can give.
O God, our Lord supreme and sovereign!

Reigning on high in regal majesty!
What can compare?
His glory outshines all the rest.
His brilliant splendor! His holiness!
Mighty power over all the earth
Filling Creation with His glorious presence
His thunderous voice heard by His powerful Word
His glory shining and overruling through our darkest despair
What can be more spectacular?
The Lord, our Master
Full of life
Omniscient and infinite, arrayed in splendor and purity
High and lifted up!
The Maker and Sustainer of all Creation
Seen in the limitless universe, galaxy upon galaxy
Showing forth God, Himself
His splendor and majesty shining forth for all to see
May we stand amazed and in awe
Breathless before His throne!
May we exalt God Almighty!
Praise and worship Him forevermore
Lord of all!
In spectacular display!

SCRIPTURES:

- I CHRONICLES 16:23-33, PSALM 96 ALL - ...worship the LORD in the splendor of his holiness..., ascribe to the LORD the glory due his name.

- I CHRONICLES 29:10-13 – Yours, O LORD, is the greatness and the power and the glory and the majesty and the splendor, for everything in heaven and earth is yours.

- PSALM 145 ALL – v.3 – Great is the LORD and most worthy of praise; his greatness no one can fathom.

- Isaiah 6 All – v.1 - …I saw the LORD seated on a throne, high and exalted, and the train of his robe filled the temple.
- Matthew 17:1-8 – There he (Christ) was transfigured before them. His face shone like the sun, and his clothes became as white as the light.
- Revelation 4 All – v.11 - … "You are worthy, our Lord and God, to receive glory and honor and power, for you created all things, and by your will they were created and have their being."

Thankful and rejoicing, for God has blessed us with freedom and peace.

Chapter 2
God's Sovereignty & Justice

DEUTERONOMY 32:3-4 – I will proclaim the name of the LORD. Oh praise the greatness of our God! He is the Rock, his works are perfect, and all his ways are just. A faithful God who does no wrong, upright and just is he.

Psalm 71:16 – I will come and proclaim your mighty acts, O Sovereign LORD; I will proclaim your righteousness, yours alone.

Preface

It's not fair! I don't understand! Why? If there is a god, why does he allow these things to happen? In today's world these are valid questions that come to mind when people face trials and difficulties. We are bombarded by wars, starvation, inhumanity and all manner of injustice. It seems like there is no justice to be found for the innocent and who above all is in control of this terrible mess we live in?

When faced with all these seemingly unanswerable questions…the only One we can look to for answers is God Almighty, Himself, because God is the only One who is completely and totally sovereign over "everything" and the only One who is just in all His ways even when we don't see or understand the situation at hand.

As we look to His Word we see a world that also had injustice in their time. I'm sure that Joseph felt betrayed, alone and forgotten with many unanswerable questions in his young life (Genesis 37, 39-40); first at the hands of his brothers who sold him into slavery in Egypt, then falsely accused by Potiphar's wife and ultimately forgotten by Pharaoh's chief cupbearer as Joseph remained in prison. And yet through all the hardship and pain, God used these tragedies in order to save his entire family during a severe famine. God is Sovereign over all things and His plans are perfect in every way… we just need to trust Him! Especially when we don't understand or waver in our faith!

And when the going gets tough and the way is hard; when life seems so unfair and people unjustly accuse and misuse us…we still need to trust Him, knowing that God truly is in control. He works all things for the good of those who love him, who have been called according to his purpose (Romans 8:28).

Of course…knowing and believing does not alter the attributes of God…He is sovereign and just no matter what. He is in control even when we don't see His hand upon the landscape. He is righteous and just, the ultimate Judge. That is His position and character; that's who He is!

By God's Orchestration

What a delightful symphony
Beyond what mankind can believe or even hope to see
A symphony in God's unerring perfection;
A wondrous, rapturous composition!
God's display of His beautiful creation;
The Lord's melodious song by His direction
The clouds skirt the spacious sky keeping pace;
The sun, moon and stars take their proper place,

The sparkling vast ocean, the mountains majesty;
God's sovereign power and glory for all to see
All life is orchestrated by the Father above;
Given to us from His heart of love

Life's rhythm and beat within His hand.
We need but agree with His perfect plan;
To participate in His glorious "band"
Needs a willing heart, obeying His commands

For God's supreme arrangement
Is performed by God alone
Our lives and very heartbeat
In tune with His rhythm and rapturous tone

We need but follow His direction;
To blend into His magnificent composition
How we listen and respond to all His loving cues;
Determine if we will obey or willingly go askew.
When we follow the Maestro's direction;
Our life will reach His total perfection.
His orchestration of our lives is for our good.

Let us seek His will and trust Him as we should

Teach us Lord to follow, adhering to Your masterful beat.
Help us Lord to intently listen until our life's complete
Your melodious orchestration is always, oh so wise.
May we follow Christ, our grand Conductor
And henceforth win our heavenly prize.

SCRIPTURES:

- JOB 36:26-37:13, 22-24 - ...God's voice thunders in marvelous ways; he does great things beyond our understanding. ...So that all men he has made may know his work,...

- PSALM 24:1-2, 10 - The earth is the Lord's, and everything in it, the world, and all who live in it; ...Who is he, this King of glory? The LORD Almighty—he is the King of glory. Selah

- ISAIAH 46:8-11 – ...I am God and there is no other...My purpose will stand. ...What I have said, that will I bring about; what I have planned, that will I do.

- ROMANS 8:28-30 – And we know that in all things God works for the good of those who love him, who have been called according to his purpose.

- II TIMOTHY 4:7-8 – I have fought the good fight, I have finished the race, I have kept the faith.

Listening to Christ, the Conductor of my life!

Hope Springs Eternal

Every week,
Every day,
Hope springs eternal
In the heart
In the soul;
Despite the circumstances,
Despite the signs of our time,
Despite catastrophes,
In the face of world threats,
Dangers and devastation,
Turmoil,
Ungodliness,
Cruelty and rebellion,
Amid upheavals in nature,
Uncertainty for the future
Still and always
Hope springs eternal!

Why?
Because of whom God is!
Sovereign and completely in control
He is the giver of life,
Sustainer in the midst,
Provider of all things good,
Lover of our heart and soul,
Eternally faithful,
Seeker of the lost,
Unwilling that any should perish,
Keeper of the found,
Forgiving of the unforgivable,
Holy, holy, holy!

> Lord God Almighty!
> So when life presses in
> Uncertainty surrounds,
> Hope springs eternal!
> In Christ it can be found.
> For whatever comes our way,
> Faith, hope and love abide.
> Hope springs eternal!
> On God we can rely!

Scriptures:

- **Psalm 62:5-6** – Find rest, O my soul, in God alone; my hope comes from him …I will not be shaken.

- **Isaiah 40:31** – But those who hope in the LORD will renew their strength. They will soar on wings like eagles; they will run and not grow weary, they will walk and not be faint.

- **I Corinthians 13:13** – And now these three remain: faith, hope and love. But the greatest of these is love.

- **Colossians 1:27** - …Christ in you, the hope of glory.

Holding onto my hope which is in Christ alone!

WHY?

It happened in the blink of an eye.
The hummingbird flying into the patio door
Unforeseen
Snuffed out in an instant
The lifeless form lying upon the ground
A faint parting flutter of the wings
Then gone!
Seconds earlier busy upon the morning air
Zooming around the bird feeder
Now no more!
In the palm of my hand beauty still evident
The tiny iridescent green feathers
The downy fluff under the wings
His beak straight and protruding
Tiny and precious
And yet the inward life no more
How sad and irreversible
The question arises
Why?
Lord you are sovereign over everything!
Why?

The great unknown question
The whys, that ever surround us
Questions unanswered, ever on our mind
Why?
For there are many things not understood!
An innocent child ill with cancer taken in infancy
Accidents and loved ones lost
Unemployment, jobs downsized
Poverty and hardship

Wars
Family splits and longtime grievances
Pain and suffering, lives in turmoil
So many questions
Oh Lord, we don't understand!
Why?
And yet in the midst of all the questions and the not knowing
You Lord remain sovereign!
We rest in who You are! For You are good!
Your ways are righteous and true!
You are unchanging in all Your ways!
You know us! You love and care for Your children!
So we trust You!
Even in the "whys" of life
Even when we don't understand
For in the midst of all our questions
You alone reign supreme!
We don't understand Your plan and purpose in it all
But we trust You and love You!
You are a good God!
Loving us and wanting us to look to You even when life is hard
May we cling to You with outstretched arms!
Following after You
And leave the "whys" in Your all-knowing hands!

SCRIPTURES:

- PSALM 25 ALL - …All the ways of the LORD are loving and faithful for those who keep the demands of his covenant.

- PSALM 71 ALL - …For you have been my hope O Sovereign LORD, my confidence since my youth. …But as for me, I will always have hope; I will praise you more and more.

- JEREMIAH 29:11-13 – For I know the plans I have for you," declares the LORD, "plans to prosper you and not to harm you, plans to give you hope and a future.

- DANIEL 4:19-37 - ...acknowledge that the Most High is Sovereign over the kingdoms of men and gives them to anyone he wishes." ...He does as he pleases with the powers of heaven and the peoples of the earth. No one can hold back his hand...praise and exalt and glorify the King of heaven, because everything he does is right and all his ways are just.

- JOHN 14:1-7 – "Do not let your hearts be troubled. Trust in God; trust also in me. ...Jesus answered, "I am the way and the truth and the life. No one comes to the Father except through me."

Trusting Sovereign God even when I don't understand

Timeless Change

Unusual weather!
Dry summer heat changed in a day
To humid sticky rainy weather
Expectant early morning sunshine clouded over
Replaced with dark threatening murky clouds
Filling the air with moisture
Waking to rumbling thunder and flashing lightning
A morning downpour splashing off rooftops onto the sidewalk
Getting the morning newspaper wet
Causing the cat to seek for cover
Not typical! A change to the day!
But a good, refreshing and unforeseen change
Keeping the temperature in check
Giving everything a summer bath
Washing off plants, watering the grass and trees
This is the day that the Lord has made
Let us rejoice and be glad in it!
Tomorrow will be different
The summer heat may return
One thing is dependable
Consistent change!

Is that not true of the life we lead?
The world in flux! Consistently changing!
The sun, moon and stars in perpetual motion
Revolving, turning, year to year
Seasons changing
Spring to summer, fall giving way to winter and back again
Life progressing
Growing older, wiser
Marrying and bearing children generation upon generation

Each day different from the last or the next
Changes in life!
And yet…there is consistency!
Consistency in the Creator of the universe!
In the One who rules over all!
God Supreme! The Sovereign King!
All-knowing, keeping life in perfect order
Eternally unchanging
Providing security and stability
Always dependable in the face of changes in our lives

When we don't understand the happenings that come upon us
When unexplained changes put our lives in turmoil
He is…always reliable and steadfast.
When heartache and tragedy change our lives forever
He is…forever merciful and caring, giving comfort.
When we become disappointed and feel unloved
His love is… unending, wrapping His arms around us.
When situations suddenly make us feel lost and alone
God's Holy Spirit, is always…near to us and within us
His very Presence directing and guiding us
When we don't think we can face another day
God alone…consistently nurtures the heart
By His Word, we are refreshed
When we have reached the end of our rope
Caught in sin and despair
He is… forever faithful providing grace and forgiveness
Changing our lives to follow in His footsteps

For God alone is transcendent and constant
He is…unchanging in all His ways.
He is… the Rock upon whom we stand.
In the face of life's changes!
He alone is… steady and unmovable

Timeless!
May we stand firmly in Christ, our Savior and Lord!

Scriptures:

- Psalm 139 All - ... All the days ordained for me were written in your book before one of them came to be.
- Ecclesiastes 3:1-15 - ...He (God) has also set eternity in the hearts of men; yet they cannot fathom what God has done from beginning to end.
- Isaiah 46:8-11 - ... I am God, and there is no other; I am God, and there is none like me.
- James 1:17-18 – Every good and perfect gift is from above, coming down from the Father of the heavenly lights, who does not change like shifting shadows...

Dependent upon God's unchanging love and grace

From this Height

Soaring high overhead, the earth is in miniature.
Cars represented by dots
Moving unnoticed along highways below
People invisible to the eye out of view and focus
Shopping malls, housing developments
Arranged in patterns and circles displayed in varied colors
Plots of ground in patchwork quilt design
Lines for main arteries and thoroughfares
Roads in straight and curvy lines
Patches of trees
Irrigated fields of green in circular shapes
Canyons and deep gullies spreading out in delicate fingers
Stream beds in serpentine shapes stretching forth
The horizon extending ever outward in all directions
The sun's glow as it breaches the distant mountains
Glistening on the lakes and rivers
Clouds floating by with misty cotton-like shapes
The contrast of expanse and smallness
From this height!

How does God view us from His Height?
From the heavens above
What does He see?
The greatness and wonder of every living soul
And yet each minute detail of our busy day
Barren ground or a fruitful life?
Directed, obedient and following His Word, His guidance?
Our pathway straight, righteous and focused on Him?
Or
Wandering, meandering and clouded by this world's demands?
Drifting and without purpose?

God sees every detail.
Every unique pattern, purpose and design in every life.
Nothing is hidden from Him!
He is omniscient, all-knowing
Ever present
All seeing
Ever watchful
He rules supreme!
He is majestic upon His throne.
Can anything hide us from His view?
What can separate us from the love of God?
We are precious in His sight.
He knows us by name.
And daily provides for our every need.
Do we wish to be seen by Him?
Or do we seek to hide ourselves?
From the One who made us?
From God Almighty!
From His Height!

Scriptures:

- **Psalm 33:8-15** - …From heaven the LORD looks down and sees all mankind; from his dwelling place he watches all who live on earth—

- **Psalm 121 All** - …The LORD watches over you—the LORD is your shade at your right hand;…

- **Psalm 139:1-18** - …Where can I go from your Spirit? Where can I flee from your presence? …When I awake, I am still with you.

- **Isaiah 6 All** - …I saw the LORD seated on a throne, high and exalted, and the train of his robe filled the temple. … "Holy, holy, holy is the LORD Almighty; the whole earth is full of his glory."

- ROMANS 8:38-39 - ...neither height nor depth...will be able to separate us from the love of God that is in Christ Jesus our Lord.

Feeling very small and insignificant but knowing God loves me above all else.

Night Sounds

You can almost hear the silence!
The quietness
The twinkle of stars in the heavens
The moon coursing across the dark sky
The calmness of night in early morning
All is peaceful and asleep, serene and still
Except the crickets chirping outside the window
The rhythmic sound piercing the silence
Heard also is the sound of cats down the street
Spatting in the distance having a feline disagreement
Noises traveling across the cool night air
Occasionally the echo of a dog's bark
Man's night watchman sounding their protective bark alarm
The noise of a freight train with the blare of its horn
Traveling from far off in the distance
Coming closer then receding into the night
A motorcycle traveling on a faraway street
Its engine heard miles away breaking the silence
The steady ticking of the bedroom clock
Marking time in the stillness
Disturbing the quiet
Night sounds!

The appearance of peace in a world of turmoil and uproar
A world oblivious to its surroundings
People living amid complacency and compromise
Unseeing, blinded by the sights and sounds of the world
The subtlety of sin
The distractions drawing them away from God
Lost in the humdrum of living
Caught in the web of technology deadening the mind and soul

The works of the enemy, Satan's deception
Piercing the world with unrest
Speaking lies to those who would listen
Disquieting the hearts of man
With wars and rumors of war
Invading, coming closer, marked by time
The fullness of the night approaching
Like a thief in the night breaking in upon the scene
Christ Cometh!
He comes to receive his own, the redeemed of the Lord!
Those who have followed and heard his call
Those who have overcome
Those who love and adore him with a whole heart
Dawn is coming!
For we shall rise to meet the Lord in the air
There will no longer be night for Christ shall be our light
The voice of the archangel, the trumpet call of God
Declaring His coming!
The heavenly host of angels giving Him glory!
Holy! Holy! Holy!
Is the Holy Lamb of God who was slain!
Are you ready?
Can you perceive what is to come, for the day approaches!
Do not be lost nor suffer God's wrath
But beware the sounds of night!

SCRIPTURES:

- DANIEL 10:4-21, 11:40-12:13 – DANIEL'S VISION – v. 12:3 – those who are wise will shine like the brightness of the heavens, and those who lead many to righteousness, like the stars for ever and ever.

- MATTHEW 24:1-25:13 - ... "watch out that no one deceives you. ...but he who stands firm to the end will be saved. ...they will see the Son of man coming on the clouds of the sky, with power and great glory. ...therefore keep watch, because you do not know the day or the hour."

- ROMANS 1:18-32 – the wrath of God is being revealed from heaven against all the godlessness and wickedness of men who suppress the truth by their wickedness,...

- I CORINTHIANS 15:12-28 – v.20 – but Christ has indeed been raised from the dead, the firstfruits of those who have fallen asleep.

- I THESSALONIANS 4:13-5:11 - ...for the Lord himself will come down from heaven...the day of the Lord will come like a thief in the night...let us be alert and self-controlled.

- REVELATION 1:7-8 – Look, he is coming with the clouds, and every eye will see him,... "I am the Alpha and the Omega," says the Lord God, "who is, and who was, and who is to come, the Almighty."

Jesus…come quickly!

"JUSTICE"

There's a hush in the courtroom.
Everyone is in attendance.
All is austere and official.
The stern judge overrules the judicious proceedings.
Court recorder tapping away
Bailiff establishing order
The jurors quiet and attentive
Attorneys prepared to hear the case.
Ready to proceed!
Innocent until proven guilty?
Probable cause
Witnesses testify and evidence given
Jury deliberations
Can justice be found?

Before the judgment seat of God!
Declared guilty before birth, unrighteous and sinful
Terrible crimes;
Slander and gossip, lust and wickedness,
Greed and depravity
Without excuse
Guilty, guilty, guilty!
Condemned and judged!
Sentenced to death!
God's justice rendered.

However a righteousness from God has been revealed!
Grace bestowed and love shown
Undeserved and freely given
Absolved of sinfulness
No longer guilty!

Declared righteous, justified before God
Glorified!
Justice has been found!
How can this be?
We have an advocate!
Righteous and holy who pleads our case before God's throne
Taking our place
Suffering our penalty and paying our punishment
He is our substitute.
We are set free being absolved of all guilt.
Justice given!

Who would do such a thing for us?
Jesus!
Jesus!
Jesus!
Wonderful Savior!
Risen Lord!
Righteous Judge!
King and Ruler over all!
Praise Him in humble gratitude!
Forevermore!

SCRIPTURES:

- JOB 16:18-21 - …even now my witness is in heaven, my advocate is on high.

- PSALM 113:4-6 - …Who is like the LORD, our God, the One who sits enthroned on high,…

- ISAIAH 59 ALL - …No one calls for justice; no one pleads his case with integrity…so justice is far from us,…The LORD looked and was displeased that there was no justice…so his own arm worked salvation for him and his own righteousness

sustained him…The Redeemer will come to Zion,…
- ROMANS 1:17 - …a righteousness from God is revealed,…
- ROMANS 1:18-32 – God's wrath revealed against mankind's godlessness and wickedness.
- ROMANS 3:23-24 - …Justified freely by his grace…
- ROMANS 5:8-9 - …we have been justified by his blood,…

So grateful for the glorious grace that Christ has given to me!

By Divine Appointment

What a travel mess!
Well-laid plans gone awry!
Flights delayed, cancellations
Engine problems, weather, ice and snow
Waiting, waiting and more waiting
Hotel and food vouchers
Making adjustments
Long slow-passing hours in the airport
Our destination delayed once again!
Frustration! Disappointment!
Why Lord? We prayed beforehand.
What is your purpose in this? Help us to see Your plan
In the midst of this storm our sight is confused, unseeing!

Finally…
Flights fall into place for God has made a way
Even…one 1st class seat!
Who will be my traveling companion?
In the seat adjacent by God's divine appointment!
Enter…a young man
Friendly, amiable and talkative
Searching and questioning
Wanting answers to life's doubts and uncertainties
Open, willing to listen
Ready to respond to the gospel message
To the call of Christ
Seeking but unsure
Not totally ready to commit and confess
However…the seed of truth has been planted

Will I ever know the result? Perhaps Not!

Perhaps only before the throne of Christ
There will be a heavenly reunion of heart and soul.
But for now…it has been by divine appointment!

How many times does God frustrate our way?
In order for His Plan and purpose to be accomplished
How do we look upon the disappointments and delays in life?
As mere inconveniences?
Rather than opportunities to be used by God
Challenges to be overcome
Looking to God's bigger picture
Knowing that God has a sovereign will
A purpose for everything that comes into our lives
Because God alone is in control!
He overrules in every situation.
We can trust him in every circumstance.
We can become God's instrument, His useful spokesperson
For He is the one who orchestrates our way
Giving us spiritual insight and a path to follow
Knowing that his plans are perfect!
Every step we take, every word we have the courage to speak
Every opportunity we use
Are by divine appointment!

Scriptures:

- Proverbs 16:9 – In his heart a man plans his course, but the LORD determines his steps.

- Proverbs 19: 21 – Many are the plans in a man's heart, but it is the LORD's purpose that prevails.

- John 3:16 – "for God so loved the world that he gave his one and only Son, that whoever believes in him shall not perish but have eternal life."

- ROMANS 8:28 – and we know that in all things God works for the good of those who love him, who have been called according to his purpose.
- GALATIANS 6:10 – therefore, as we have opportunity, let us do good to all people, especially to those who belong to the family of believers.
- COLOSSIANS 4:2-6 – …let your conversation be always full of grace, seasoned with salt, so that you may know how to answer everyone.
- I TIMOTHY 6:11-16 – God, the blessed and only Ruler, the Kings of kings and Lord of lords,…to him be honor and might forever. Amen.

Praying that Andrew, "Andy", would seek and know the love of Jesus

In the Map room of the Almighty

It was a hurtful thing
An act unworthy of the bearer
Unexpected
Harsh
Unfeeling
Done without compassion
Lacking of love for another
Unjustified
Beyond comprehension
How and why?
So many unanswered questions
Unbelievable
How could this be happening?
This was a person that was trusted
A person of high standing
One who was respected
But this was an act of betrayal
Cowardice
An unwise decision
But made just the same
A choice!
A new direction
Down a different pathway
In the map room of the Almighty!
Before God and man
And yet
The course had been charted
The path had been taken
But

In the face of injustice
God is still sovereign!
For he knows the plans he has for us
And they are for good!
We may not see the good at the present time
But God is a God of grace and love
Able to uphold those in need
To comfort those who mourn
Able to bring good out of chaos
Joy out of heartbreak
God is in control of all things
He ultimately sets our course
According to the choices we make
And there are many choices to be made in life
Either for good
Or bad!
And the consequences of those choices
Are
Either good
Or bad!
That we would always choose God's best!
Help us Lord to choose your way!
And when we have been unwise
That we would return to your loving arms
For God is gracious and forgiving
Desiring to lead us onward
To lead us to Himself
In the map room of the Almighty!
Where God resides!

Scriptures:

- Psalm 66 All – v.7- He rules forever by his power, his eyes watch the nations—let not the rebellious rise up against him. Selah

- Isaiah 40:10 – See, the Sovereign LORD comes with power, and his arm rules for him. See, his reward is with him, and his recompense accompanies him.
- Jeremiah 29:11 – for I know the plans I have for you," declares the LORD, "plans to prosper you and not to harm you, plans to give you hope and a future."
- Jeremiah 31 all – … "I have loved you with an everlasting love; I have drawn you with loving-kindness.

God is good and sovereign over all!

Chapter 3
God's Grace

ROMANS 3:23-24 – for all have sinned and fall short of the glory of God, and are justified freely by his grace through the redemption that came by Christ Jesus.

EPHESIANS 2:8-9 – For it is by grace you have been saved, through faith—and this not from yourselves, it is the gift of God—not by works, so that no one can boast.

Preface

Grace…wondrous grace…undeserved favor! Grace is what everyone wants to be shown but so often they are unwilling to show it to others. God's grace goes far beyond the grace that you might extend to someone you know. God's grace is given even when we don't deserve it and oft-times even when we don't merit it.

I know that I look back on my life and see times of regret and lost opportunities and there have been lots of times that I could have done or gone in a different direction. There have been times of remorse over bad attitudes, harsh and angry words, wrong thoughts and actions. I would hope that in all the areas where I have failed in the past, grace might be given and I would be forgiven. I could chalk it up to…oh, well! What difference does it make…it's in the past. However…we have an all-seeing God, who observes all that we do or say, even think or feel. God sees all and knows all, past, present and future. We live in a sinful world and we are part of that sinful society with a sin nature and personal sins of our own. So what do we do with all those sins, the regret and remorse that we feel? Where do we go to be absolved of the sorrow and regret that we carry?

Only God is able to provide grace and a way of salvation and forgiveness that "erases" the sins we bear; for God looks at us and our life of sin through the filter of His Son, Jesus Christ! There is grace to be found through the sacrificial blood of Christ shed on the Cross for the sins of the world. Shed for us! Grace has been shown to us through Christ's sacrifice which takes away the sin that we bear. Grace, grace, wondrous grace has taken away the penalty of my sin and yours. So…when God looks upon me and my life…He sees the sacrifice that Christ has paid for me and I hence forth am regarded as "not guilty" before the throne of God. Amazing!

There is only one requirement…we need to come and believe in God's Son, Christ Jesus for our salvation and follow after Him in our daily life. Have you put your trust in Him and what He has done for you? What amazing grace God has given to us! Thanks be to God, the only truly Gracious One!

— Alive —

They reach skyward like arms stretched out wide
Dark barren sticks of wood and bark
Branches weathered by winter cold
Completely dead in appearance
The tree's life-giving sap lying dormant beneath the ground
Until spring's awakening comes forth
Warmth and sun and longer days
Slowly, gradually, yet almost overnight emerging
The touch of life breaks forth with flowering buds
With delicate petals opening, one by one
Cascading gently to the ground like snow
Tiny slivers of chartreuse green leafing out along each branch
Responding to the sun's warming rays
Dormant trees coming to life emerging from winter's sleep
Plum trees dressed in soft white lace
Apples arrayed in blossoms of white and pink
Flowering peach trees covered in stunning rosy clusters
Bedecked in their finest garb
Bringing forth their blossoms and greenery
Pollinated by busy bees flitting from flower to flower
A subtle sweet aroma filling the springtime air
Steadily growing, maturing , producing luscious fruit in season
Alive!
Resurrection life! Easter Day life!
New life from what was once dead
Christ's resurrection from the tomb
He is risen! He is risen indeed!
He who was put to death with outstretched arms upon the cross
Laid bare upon stark wooden beams
Scorned and put to shame
Abandoned to the darkness of the grave

Shut into the depths of the earth
Experiencing death for us
Christ, our Sacrifice
"HE IS ALIVE!"
Overcoming death, risen to new life
Crowned with glory and majesty and garbed in royal robes
Alive and reigning at the right hand of the Father
Bringing forth the message of Easter
Salvation and new life in Christ for those who are lost!
For those who are without God in their life
Barren, lost, dead in sin
Existing in a dormant life, buried and unused
A life with outstretched arms in need of a Savior
Weathered by life's disappointments and failures
Living apart from God, soiled with sin and regret
Apart from the One who loves them with an everlasting love.
Resurrection life! Available to all who believe!
Those who were dead in their sin are made alive in Christ!
Through the touch of Almighty God
By the power of the Holy Spirit
By grace and faith in Christ Jesus, our Lord
Eternal life He gives!
Forever made alive!
Hallelujah! Praise to the Lord, our King of kings!
Will "you" choose to believe in Christ and follow Him?

Scriptures:

- Matthew 28:1-10; Mark 16:1-11; Luke 24:1-12 and John 20:1-18 – "Why do you look for the living among the dead? He is not here; he has risen!

- Luke 15:11-32 – v.24 – For this son of mine was dead and is alive again; he was lost and is found.

- JOHN 11:25-26 – Jesus said to her, "I am the resurrection and the life. He who believes in me will live, even though he dies; and whoever lives and believes in me will never die. Do you believe this?"
- ROMANS 6:1-14 – v. 11 –In the same way, count yourselves dead to sin but alive to God in Christ Jesus….offer yourselves to God, as those who have been brought from death to life;…
- EPHESIANS 2:1-10 – But because of his great love for us, God, who is rich in mercy, made us alive with Christ even when we were dead in transgressions—it is by grace you have been saved…it is the gift of God.
- I CORINTHIANS 15 ALL – v. 22 – For as in Adam all die, so in Christ all will be made alive.

Made alive in Christ…Praise the Lord!

-CLEAN-

The wind made a terrible mess!
Leaves, dust and dirt blowing everywhere
Floating on the air, landing in the water of the swimming pool
Sinking to the bottom
Drifts of sand clinging to the side walls
Making dunes of silt with all the other debris
What a mess!
Needing a thorough cleaning
And along came Stephanie!
With her brushes, hoses, net and pole
Scooping out the clutter, brushing the side walls
Vacuuming the bottom, cleaning the tile and filter
Checking the chemicals and adding the chlorine
What an amazing transformation!
Sparkling and crystal clear
The sun casting diamonds upon the water
The gentle breeze making ripples across the liquid surface
The bottom and walls clear and spotless
Inviting!
Come and swim! The water is great!
For I am "clean"!

To be clean! Impossible in this life!
We are surrounded by the winds of this world.
The pollution of sin and filth
Floating on the air of our everyday life
A world of corruption and chaos, war and rumors of wars
Drifts of all manner of sinful deeds
The debris of a sinful nature
What a mess!
We need a thorough cleaning!

A cleansing from our sin! A transformation!
And along came Christ with his perfect sacrifice!
As the spotless pure Lamb of God
That takes away the sin of the world
Sacrificed upon the Cross
Resurrected in victory over sin and death
Scooping out the clutter of our lives
Brushing away the guilt of our sinful acts
Vacuuming away the past and cleansing the heart within
We are washed in the blood of the Lamb
Checked and rechecked in the innermost parts
By His indwelling Holy Spirit
What an amazing transformation!
We stand clean and righteous before a mighty God!
Wearing the robes of Christ's righteousness
Sparkling clear and clean before the throne of grace
Basking in the presence of the Holy One
Invited to the wedding banquet of the Lamb
As the bride of Christ, our Bridegroom
The Son of the Most High!
Come!
God's invitation is for you!
You may boldly approach the throne of grace!
For you are "clean"!

SCRIPTURES:

- PSALM 51:1-17 – …Wash away all my iniquity and cleanse me from my sin…wash me, and I will be whiter than snow… Restore to me the joy of your salvation…

- I CORINTHIANS 6:9-11 – Do you not know that the wicked will not inherit the kingdom of God? …But you were washed, you were sanctified, you were justified in the name of the Lord Jesus Christ and by the Spirit of our God.

- Ephesians 5:25-27 - ...Christ loved the church and gave himself up for her to make her holy, cleansing her by the washing with water through the word, and to present her to himself as a radiant church, without stain or wrinkle or any other blemish, but holy and blameless.
- Hebrews 10:19-25 - ...let us draw near to God with a sincere heart in full assurance of faith, having our hearts sprinkled to cleanse us from a guilty conscience and having our bodies washed with pure water.
- I Peter 1:13-2:3 - ... "Be holy, because I am holy." ...you were redeemed...with the precious blood of Christ, a lamb without blemish or defect....and so your faith and hope are in God.

So grateful for the salvation I have in Christ!

Out of the Darkness

The night enveloped and wrapped in darkness
No light to be found in the blackness above
Searching in the expansive sky
Has even the moon disappeared?
Scanning the heavens
But through the pine trees, a glimmer
Peeking through the dark branches
A crescent of brightness somewhat hidden and obscure
But as I move aside
My view unobstructed and made clear
The moon shines forth in radiance
Clearly shining in splendor out of the heavenly expanse
A pathway of brilliance like sparkling diamonds upon a pond
Unhindered by the dark night
Not deterred by the trees
Bringing light out of darkness!
By God's design?
Absolutely!
According to His plan and purpose
For God is the Creator and Sustainer of all things
The heavens declare His glory
The moon and the stars
In radiance, they shine out of the darkness of night
And so it is in our lives also!
For in the midst of the darkness that surrounds us
The world of injustice and strife
Out of heartache and pain, difficulties and distress
Out of the blackness of a sinful world all around
Came a Light!
Jesus!
The Light of the world!

The hope and salvation of mankind
For we were enveloped and wrapped in darkness
There was no remedy for our sinful state
No clear pathway to our God
But…Jesus!
Made our way clear
His Light shines in the darkness
His death and resurrection have saved us!
We now can come to the throne of grace
Like sparkling diamonds
Wrapped in Christ's robes of righteousness
Unhindered
Not deterred by our sinful nature
Coming into the Light
Coming out of the darkness into His glorious presence
By God's design

Will you not praise your Lord and Savior?
The One who has redeemed you!
The gracious One!
Who has brought you into His wonderful Light.
Out of darkness!

Scriptures:

- GENESIS 1:1-5, 14-19 – And God said, "Let there be light," and there was light.

- PSALM 19 ALL – v.1- The heavens declare the glory of God; the skies proclaim the work of his hands.

- PSALM 139 ALL – v.12 - …even the darkness will not be dark to you; the night will shine like the day, for darkness is as light to you.

- ISAIAH 60:1-3 – "Arise, shine, for your light has come, and the glory of the LORD rises upon you.

- JOHN 1:1-5 - ...The light shines in the darkness, but the darkness has not understood it.
- JOHN 8:12 - ...he (Jesus) said, "I am the light of the world. Whoever follows me will never walk in darkness, but will have the light of life."
- I JOHN 1:5-10 - ...But if we walk in the light, as he is in the light, we have fellowship with one another, and the blood of Jesus, his Son, purifies us from all sin.

Lord let me stay within Your light!

RUBY RED

The foliage is stunning
New spring growth
Where only a barren root base resided
Severe trimming coming to life
Ruby red shoots
Emerging from cut-back rosebush canes
Shining crimson with a glistening luster
Leaves quickly turning to tinges of dark vibrant green
Edged in ruby red brilliance
Wax coated
Repelling early morning droplets of dew
Leaves growing, protruding outward
Rising to the warming sun
Losing their ruby red hues
But developing buds of blossoms
Blooms growing upward on straight stems
Fashioned with prickly thorns
Finally
Blossoming in glorious beauty
God's ruby red foliage
Turned to roses of early spring perfection!

What color do you imagine?
When thoughts bring you to the Cross of Christ?
The color of the barren rough-hewed cross
A cut-down and dead discarded tree
Brown turned to ruby red
By the blood of the Lamb
Shed for the forgiveness of sins
Without glory
Costly

Untold pain and suffering
Ruby red!
Covered in the blood of a dying Messiah!
Wrapped in a crown of thorns
But out of that starkness
The ultimate conquering King!
Risen and coming again!
Ruby red!
Christ's compelling life
The Savior of the world
Given for the lost
From the love of a Father's hands
With compassion and mercy
The means of salvation for all who believe
Trusting in Him alone
Ruby red!
The precious blood of Christ
Welling up unto eternal life
Growing in believing hearts
To those who seek to follow
Ruby red!
Blossoming
Producing beauty
Giving life and hope
Bringing glory to a glorious God who reigns on high
Ruby red!
Praise to His holy name!

SCRIPTURES:

- ISAIAH 53 ALL – v.6-We all, like sheep, have gone astray, each of us has turned to his own way; and the LORD has laid on him the iniquity of us all.

- SONG OF SOLOMON 2:1-15 – I am a rose of Sharon, a lily of the valley…his banner over me is love.

- ROMANS 3:21-26 – v.25- God presented him (Christ) as a sacrifice of atonement through faith in his blood.
- HEBREWS 9:11-28 - …without the shedding of blood there is no forgiveness.
- HEBREWS 12:2-3 – Let us fix our eyes on Jesus, …who for the joy set before him endured the cross,…
- I PETER 1:18-21 - …you were redeemed…with the precious blood of Christ, a lamb without blemish or defect.

Awed by Christ's sacrifice for me and so grateful for it

"Monopoly" Grace

Go to jail, go directly to jail!
Do not pass go. Do not collect $200.00
"Monopoly's" detention space!
Stay in jail?
Wait out your turn? Pay the price or roll the dice?
When you don't have the fee, the hefty price
There is no freedom.
There are no guarantees on the next roll of the dice.
You may land in jail once again!
And again, and again
Is there no end to this game?
But…if you have a "get out of jail free" card!
Voila! Out of jail on your next turn
And on your way, ready to play the game once again
"Get out of jail, free!"
Don't we all want to possess that card?
Even when you don't need it at the time
Save it and keep it for the possibility of going to jail.
Don't trade it, keep it handy.
For when you have no funds to set yourself free
"Get out of jail free" "Monopoly" grace!

What about "real" life?
Where do you feel imprisoned, "in jail"?
Bound and entangled, ensnared and in chains
Held in circumstances not your own
Caught in the grip of sin and despair
Unable to set yourself free
Life is not a game!
But imprisonment of the heart and soul is real!
It easily grips our lives holding us fast

Capturing us, immobilizing us
Over and over again!
We are held captive
Satan has chained us and bound us
Is there no freedom from the power of sin and death?
Voila! There is a "Get out of jail free" card!
Christ Jesus, our Lord!
He has paid the price
He's made the ultimate sacrifice
But not without much suffering and pain
He has saved us with his very blood, his life.
At the Cross He paid the cost of our sin.
Setting the captives free…Free indeed!
Giving us grace and pardon
Bringing new life to those who believe
Redeeming us from the power of sin and death
Saving us from bondage
Providing Holy Spirit power to live victoriously
Giving us hope and a future
Eternal life forever!

Will we thank and praise him?
Will we follow and obey Him?
Oh, so great a salvation!
The wondrous grace we've been given
Which goes far beyond "Monopoly" grace!

Scriptures:

- Isaiah 61:1-3 - …He has sent me to bind up the brokenhearted, to proclaim freedom for the captives and release from darkness for the prisoners,…

- John 8:31-36 – So if the Son sets you free, you will be free indeed.

- ROMANS 3:23-25 – for all have sinned and fall short of the glory of God, and are justified freely by his grace through the redemption that came by Christ Jesus.
- ROMANS 5:8-9 – but God demonstrates his own love for us in this: while we were still sinners, Christ died for us.
- ROMANS 8:1-17 – Therefore, there is now no condemnation for those who are in Christ Jesus, because through Christ Jesus the law of the spirit of life set me free from the law of sin and death.
- EPHESIANS 2:1-10 - …for it is by grace you have been saved, through faith—and this not from yourselves, it is a gift of God…
- I PETER 2:18-25 - …He himself bore our sins in his body on the tree, so that we might die to sins and live for righteousness; by his wounds you have been healed.

Thanks be to God for his amazing grace!

White as Snow

Soaring high overhead on eagle's wings
Ultra white snow covering the surface below
Sparkling and bedecked in shimmering diamonds
In the brilliant sunlight
Its stunning whiteness blinding the eyes
Blanketing everything in a chilling winter's sleep
Covering firs, pines and spruce
Bending their boughs downward to the ground
Melting them into the landscape
Clinging to lamp posts and barren tree branches
Crevices, mountain peaks, roads and highways
Packed in serpentine snowdrifts
Resembling sand dunes made of soft winter fluffiness
Everything hidden in Rocky Mountain wonder
Mesas barely visible captured in frigid coldness
Only azure lakes break the stark whiteness
Icing over into translucent opaqueness
Clouds grasp the higher snowy peaks
More whiteness blending into snow's scenery
Encapsulated and encrusted into white obscurity
Pure and clean
Dazzling and held encased in timeless beauty
Captured in calm splendor and majesty
Serene and peaceful
In quiet hush
A winter wonderland
White as snow!

Beyond the obvious
Beyond what can be seen and felt
God reigns supreme over all!

In holy righteousness
Taking our broken and stained lives
Our filthy rags of mere existence and emptiness
Transforming them by His powerful Word
Christ Jesus, the One who can save us!
Transforming us by His righteousness and purity
Changing our lives forever!
Can we not see that our very being is so incomplete
Without worth, without Christ residing within us?
We are so unrighteous and unholy?
Needing a covering
Needing cleansing and purification
By His precious saving blood
Transposing His purity and cleanliness
Making us acceptable in His sight
Making us whiter than snow
Holy and pure
Cleansing us from all unrighteousness
Filling us with Himself
Through His abiding Holy Spirit
Displaying us as sparkling gems in our Savior's crown
Dressed in robes of purest white
Before our Holy Righteous God!
White as snow!

SCRIPTURES:

- LEVITICUS 20:7 - …I am the LORD, who makes you holy.

- PSALM 51:1-12 - …wash me, and I will be whiter than snow… Create in me a pure heart, O God, and renew a steadfast spirit within me,….

- ISAIAH 1:18-20 - … "Though your sins are like scarlet, they shall be as white as snow; though they are red as crimson, they shall be like wool."

- Isaiah 64:6 – All of us have become like one who is unclean, and all our righteous acts are like filthy rags;...
- II Timothy 4:7-8 – Now there is in store for me the crown of righteousness, which the Lord, the righteous Judge, will award to me on that day—
- I Peter 1:15-16 – But just as he who called you is holy, so be holy in all you do; for it is written: "Be holy, because I am holy."
- Revelation 7:9-17 - ...They were wearing white robes... These are they who have come out of the great tribulation; they have washed their robes and made them white in the blood of the Lamb.

Marveling in God's righteousness available to me, through Christ, my Lord

Still Alive

It hardly seems possible!
After the treacherous fall winds
After the pomegranate tree had completely blown over
Lying motionless upon the ground
Limbs and branches broken off
Leaves withering and falling brown all around
And yet…a cause to hope
The taproot seemed intact, albeit bent and exposed
But holding fast and secure in the soil
So…after up-righting the poor lifeless tree
Trimming the broken dead branches
Securing it firmly with stakes and supports
Watering profusely, fertilizing generously
Then waiting, waiting, waiting
Through winter's dormancy for spring's warm awakening
And then…as if overnight
Tiny bits of stunning green emerging along the branches
Leaves of life shining brightly in the morning light
The tree has survived, growing forth in splendor
With promise of fruitfulness once again
Still alive!

God's wondrous grace even when everything seems lost!
When our life seems turned upside down
Blown over by hard times
When we feel undone and defeated, withering in the light of day
Tired and falling apart amid the circumstances of life
It hardly seems possible!
There is still cause to hope!
Even when we are broken Christ holds us secure in His love!
We are upheld, safe within His arms

No matter the circumstance!
For He uses this time to grow us in our faith
To depend upon Him as our sure and steady Rock
Causing us to seek His face in prayer before the throne of grace
To be fed by His Word and nurtured by His Holy Spirit
Emerging stronger in our faith in Him
Growing bit by bit
Able to walk in the sunshine once again
Being fruitful in service
For…we are still alive!
In Him there is life!
For He is the Light of men!
Once we were lost but God in His grace has saved us
Christ died so that we might live.
Arise!
Give praise to the One who has saved you!
The Righteous One!
Worthy of all our praise!
Arise and walk in newness of life!
Once you were lost and dead in sin.
But now you are…
Alive in Christ!

Scriptures:

- PSALMS 1 ALL - …He (the man who is blessed) is like a tree planted by streams of water, which yields its fruit in season and whose leaf does not wither. Whatever he does prospers.

- PSALM 68:19-20 - …Our God is a God who saves; from the Sovereign LORD comes escape from death.

- LUKE 19:10 – "For the Son of Man came to seek and to save what was lost."

- JOHN 3:16 – For God so loved the world that he gave his one and only Son, that whoever believes in him shall not perish but have eternal life.

- ROMANS 6:1-14 - ...count yourselves dead to sin but alive in God in Christ Jesus.
- II CORINTHIANS 5:17 – Therefore, if anyone is in Christ, he is a new creation; the old has gone, the new has come!
- EPHESIANS 2:1-12 - ...But because of his great love for us, God, who is rich in mercy, made us alive with Christ even when we were dead in transgressions—it is by grace you have been saved.

Thank you Lord, that I am alive in You!

Behind the Veil

They are delightful creatures.
Furry, frisky, fun to watch raccoons!
Hiding behind their black mask peeking out into the forest world
Blending in with their surroundings
Showing up at back doors of houses and cabins
Scavengers by nature scratching for handouts
Digging in the earth and snow with sharp claws and teeth
Finding food by night, washing it with care before they eat
Their bushy striped ringed tail bobbing up and down
Playfully climbing trees hiding in treetops
Precariously walking along the upper branches
Teetering on the ridges of fences and walls
Finding a cozy den for their young safe and snug
A place protected from the elements within God's creation
Raccoons behind the mask!

Is not all of life a mystery?
Hidden behind the mask of uncertainty, indecision and choices
Behind the veil of the unknown
One might think so!
But be assured God has a set purpose
A perfect plan for each and every life
And we can know the will of the Lord
Comprehend and hear the words of God
For Christ has made a way for us through the veil
Behind the curtain of his temple
Providing access to our heavenly Father above
Straight before the throne of God
How can we truly know the mysteries of life?
All that God is and the essence of his character
How can we know the will of the Father above?

We have only breached the surface as revealed in His Holy Word
He is majestic and hidden from our sight
But to those who love Him and are called according to His will
God makes Himself known in part
We see but through a mirror dimly
Revelation by His Holy Spirit
Creation also revealing His majesty, might and beauty!
Above all, revealed in his beloved Son
God's very essence of who He is
Jesus Christ, our Lord!
For behind the veil
We have received God's love and grace
A oneness with God
Walking in fellowship with our glorious Lord and Savior
Within His presence where there is security
Our eternal home, a place of rest and repose
Cleansed and redeemed by Christ's very blood
Nurtured and feed by His Word
Drinking at springs of everlasting water
Protected, safe and snug forevermore
Loved beyond measure! Behind the veil!

SCRIPTURES:

- EXODUS 26:31-35 – …the curtain will separate the Holy Place from the Most Holy Place.

- MATTHEW 27:45-56 - …at that moment the curtain of the temple was torn in two from top to bottom.

- LUKE 23:44-49 - …for the sun stopped shining. And the curtain of the temple was torn in two

- JOHN 4:4-26 - …whoever drinks the water I give him will never thirst. Indeed, the water I give him will become in him a spring of water welling up to eternal life.

- II Corinthians 3:7-18 - …and we, who with unveiled faces all reflect the Lord's glory, are being transformed into his likeness with ever increasing glory, which comes from the Lord, who is the Spirit.
- Hebrews 4 All - …let us, therefore, make every effort to enter that rest,…therefore, since we have a great high priest who has gone through the heavens, Jesus the Son of God, let us hold firmly to the faith we profess. …let us then approach the throne of grace with confidence, so that we may receive mercy and find grace to help us in our time of need.
- Hebrews 10:19-25 – therefore, brothers, since we have confidence to enter the Most Holy Place by the blood of Jesus, by a new and living way opened for us through the curtain, that is, his body…let us draw near to God with a sincere heart in full assurance of faith,…

Thank you Jesus for providing the way of salvation!

Morning Grace

A cacophony of chattering birdsong greets the day.
The soothing sound of a mourning dove
cooing in the tall pine tree.
A hummingbird flits among the bottlebrush blossoms
gathering sweet nectar along the way.
A brisk chill to the start of the day
A freshness to the morning air
A soft breeze in the treetops causing the leaves to gently flutter
Dewdrops from a dense fog glue themselves to the landscape,
Kissing the roses and their glossy foliage
Slowly the earth awakens giving rise to the radiant sunshine.
Parting the clouds and fog
Bringing warmth to the landscape
Has not God graced us with His love?
Blessing us with His wondrous Creation?
Flowers and birds and trees
All working in melodious harmony!
God's morning grace!

God's grace is abundant, showered down upon us.
Undeserved favor extended our way
Yet we continually take it for granted
Not stopping to seek Him or pray?
For His mercies are new every morning
His grace, sufficient for each new day
Does not God's grace shine down upon us?
Like soft moon glow on a star-filled night?
Blessing us with His love and mercy
Touching everything within His sight!

Every Day…God "graces" us…with His unfailing love
> *Psalm 32:10*

Having compassion and comfort for those who are lost
> *Isaiah 49:13*
> *II Corinthians 1:3-7*

Daily giving us protection and safety
> *Psalm 91:14-15*

Provision without cost
> *I Timothy 6:17*

Giving us His Holy Word, the Bible
> *II Timothy 3:16-17*

God's Spirit to show us the way
> *Ephesians 2:18*

His guidance and direction so we don't go astray
> *Psalm 25:4-6*

Forgiveness without measure by His redeeming Son
> *Colossians 1:13-14*

Salvation and eternal life by Christ's death for us hath won.
> *Hebrews 5:7-9*

Have we become complacent?
Forgetting the benefits we have received?
For God has truly "graced us" beyond what we can merely see
Will we not thank Him for His provisions?
Will we not daily draw close and on Him rely?
For as we rise at the start of each new day
God will meet us as we travel on our way.
He is our guide and constant companion
Caring for us beyond what we can fathom
Will you desire to seek Him in the morning quiet?
To come and see what He requires.
For God's morning grace comes right where you are
His love reaching down from beyond the stars
Will you seek Him face to face?
And thank Him for His saving grace!

Lamentations 3:21-26, 32 – Yet this I call to mind and therefore I have hope; because of the Lord's great love we are not consumed, for his compassions never fail. They are new every morning; great is your faithfulness. …so great is his unfailing love.

So grateful for the grace the Lord has given to me.

Eclipse

In the dark of night
A stillness; tranquil silence and peace
The sky above in deepest ebony
With twinkling stars piercing the expanse
The milky white moon!
A glowing orb of radiance shining brightly
In fullest splendor illuminating the landscape
And then it begins, bit by bit!
The shadow of the earth traverses over the moon's surface.
Hiding the sun's glowing light; and so it continues
The arc of light growing ever smaller and thinner
The shadow traveling, creeping ever forward until all is obscure
Or is it?
For there remains a glowing of reflective light coming forth
The moon is "not" obliterated, only in subtle shadow.
A "Blood Moon" of beautiful orange-red, with a glorious glow!
The full eclipse is realized!
And gradually, the moon reemerges once again
Shining forth with full dazzling light in the dark night sky!
How wondrous is God's creation!
And so it was meant to be!
God's creation was made perfect and good from time's beginning
The sun, moon and stars, radiant and shining forth
All of creation made by the hand of the sovereign Creator
Pure, spotless and without blemish
Then sin darkened the scene
A shadow of turning from perfection spoiling its pristine beauty
A wandering away from God's perfect plan, bit by bit
Mankind traversed away from God in disobedience
Going their own way; taking their own path
Leaving the "way" that God intended

Penetrating our world today in sinfulness
God is obscure and not seen, pushed into the background
Hidden in the shadows of the mind and soul
However, all is not lost!
For the Light of God has been revealed!
Christ Jesus, our Lord!
His precious blood and sacrifice has made a way of hope
Overcoming the shadow of the Cross
Alone and seemingly abandoned by God
Our pure, spotless Redeemer
Taking upon Himself, our sin and reproach
The pierced, sinless, and perfect Lamb of God!
Emerging in glory and splendor
Out of the darkness of the grave
Death's grip could not hold Him nor overcome Him
Christ arose victorious!
He shines in brilliance, splendor and glory!
Our Light shining in the darkness! Our salvation!
Reigning at the right hand of the Father
All praise and glory to our gracious and loving Savior!
May Christ Jesus be glorified!

SCRIPTURES:

- GENESIS 1:1-5,14-19 - …And God said, "Let there be light," and there was light…God made…the lesser light to govern the night. He made the stars…And God saw that it was good.

- PSALM 23 ALL - … though I walk through the valley of the shadow of death, I will fear no evil, for you are with me;…

- ISAIAH 53 ALL - …But he was pierced for our transgressions… by his wounds we are healed. …The LORD has laid on him the iniquity of us all.

- MATTHEW 27:26-50 - …From the sixth hour until the ninth

hour darkness came over all the land. ...Jesus cried out in a loud voice, "...My God, my God, why have you forsaken me?"

- MATTHEW 28:1-10 - ...He is not here; he has risen, just as he said.

- ROMANS 1:17 – For in the gospel a righteousness from God is revealed, a righteousness that is by faith from first to last, just as it is written: "The righteous will live by faith."

- I PETER 1:5-10 - ...God is light; in him there is no darkness at all. ...But if we walk in the light, as he is in the light,... the blood of Jesus, His Son, purifies us from all sin.

- REVELATION 21 ALL - ...The city does not need the sun or the moon to shine on it, for the glory of God gives it light, and the Lamb is its lamp.

May Christ be glorified! He has risen indeed!

Unchanging Grace

Yesterday the sky was clear
Early morning brilliance overhead
Crystal clear images in the heavens above
A vibrant full moon, stunning against the blackness of night
Shining forth with glorious light
Stars sparkling, twinkling in quiet stillness
Shouting forth their presence before the break of day
Supreme beauty surrounding the earth below
A stillness and coolness filling the morning air
But that was yesterday!
Today is different.
A mist and cloudiness have overwhelmed the morning
Blanketing the sky with a dreary heaviness
Dew fills the air with moisture
Watery droplets cling to the blades of grassy lawn
No moon, nor stars today!
All is hidden from view beyond the overcast morning
But the heavens still remain as before in the upper atmosphere
Ever glowing overhead, beyond the fog and haze
All things are held together by God's strong and mighty hand!
By His supreme sovereignty! By God's unchanging grace!
So, why do we question or doubt God in any way?
When things are not going as we had planned
When the mist and the fog overwhelm our day
Obscuring God's wondrous grace from sight
Yesterday we had so much clarity, joy and presence of mind!
All was going well and perfect
And then…a difficulty came along!
What happened to the faith in which we were walking?
The dependency and clear vision we had in the Lord?
Listening to the still small voice of the Holy Spirit

Taking each step in the light of God's Word
What caused us to doubt?
Leading us in a different direction and overwhelming our day
Causing us to be depressed, downhearted and discouraged
Unsure of which path to take
Wandering aimlessly without purpose
What is clouding our way?
What is obscuring our view of our glorious God?
And yet…deep down inside
We know that God is always there and sovereign over all.
We know the truth of His Word
He holds all things together by His mighty hand!
Have we forgotten who exactly He is?
The One who reigns supreme over all the earth!
Abounding in love and mercy
Able to save and uphold and protect those whom He loves
He is our great Provider, gracing us with His constant care
An ever-present help in time of trouble
He has saved us by His grace
Each day, He graces us with His presence
Where is our cause to doubt Him?
He will never leave us nor forsake us!
He is unchanging in His love for us.
Turn your eyes toward Him and wholeheartedly thank Him!
For His unchanging grace to you!

Scriptures:

- Deuteronomy 31:6-8 – "…The LORD himself goes before you and will be with you; he will never leave you nor forsake you. Do not be afraid; do not be discouraged."

- Psalm 46 All – God is our refuge and strength, an ever-present help in trouble.

- Isaiah 33:2 – O LORD, be gracious to us; we long for you. Be our strength every morning, our salvation in time of distress.

- MALACHI 3:6-7 – "I the LORD do not change. ...Return to me, and I will return to you," says the LORD Almighty.
- EPHESIANS 2:4-10 - ...For it is by grace you have been saved, through faith—and this not from yourselves, it is the gift of God—not by works, so that no one can boast.
- HEBREWS 12:22-29 - ...Therefore, since we are receiving a kingdom that cannot be shaken, let us be thankful, and so worship God acceptably with reverence and awe, for our "God is a consuming fire."
- JAMES 1:16-18 - ...Every good and perfect gift is from above, coming down from the Father of the heavenly lights, who does not change like shifting shadows.

Resting in the unchanging grace of God Almighty!

Mud Puddle

Little boy with a water hose
Dirt pile plus water
Mix together!
Mud puddle fun!
A little more water needed for stirring and mixing
Chocolaty muddy brown water
Gooey, sticky mud everywhere!
Feet stamping, mud flying in all directions
Compacted into balls
Letting the mud ooze through small fingers
Throwing clods and clumps
More water
Smearing the mixture all over
Hands brown, legs and arms splattered
More water
Having fun in the mud puddle
Cheap entertainment
Wiping hands on shirt and pants to get clean
But a bath and soap is required
No other way to be clean again.
But…oh the fun while it lasted

Man's dilemma
The mud puddle of life
"SIN!"
Add man's desire to do things his way.
Sin becomes gooey, sticky
It captures you.
At first, it's mere dirt
A spot, a blemish upon our righteousness before God
But we add water so to speak

Continuing to go in our own direction
Desiring pleasures for a time
Captured in sin's grip ignoring God and His ways
Man's sin and rebellion
Mud flying touching others
Getting dirtier
The apparent fun of it all!
But with no hope of getting clean
A bath is required!

God's Remedy!
Christ Jesus, God's Only Son
Pure and holy
Sent to save the world from the stain and grip of sin.
Washed in the blood of the Lamb
Cleansed by His righteousness, made whiter than snow
Justified by faith and made right with God
Pleasing to Him with a sweet aroma!
Jesus, our Savior and Salvation!
Mankind's Redeemer and righteousness!
Why would we not choose to come to Him?

Scriptures:

- Isaiah 1:18-20 - ... "Though your sins are like scarlet, they shall be as white as snow,…"

- Matthew 1:21 - …you are to give him the name Jesus, because he will save his people from their sins."

- Acts 2:38-39 - … "Repent and be baptized, every one of you, in the name of Jesus Christ for the forgiveness of your sins.

- Acts 4:12 – Salvation is found in no one else, for there is no other name under heaven given to men by which we must be saved."

- ROMANS 1:17 - ... "The righteous will live by faith."
- ROMANS 1:18-32 - ...For although they knew God, they neither glorified him as God nor gave thanks to him,... They exchanged the truth of God for a lie,...
- I CORINTHIANS 6:9-11 - ...But you were washed, you were sanctified, you were justified in the name of the Lord Jesus Christ and by the Spirit of our God.

We all need a Savior!

Out of the Shadow

A jewel jutting skyward toward the heavens
Stark, strong and immoveable
Made of hard granite
Coming into view with the rising sun
Still obscure in part
Hidden within the hazy shadows of early morning
Rocks and crevices barely visible in blues and purples
Yet the peaks ablaze in the breaking sunlight
Ever growing in brilliance
The sun working its presence ever downward
Creeping slowly along the hard granite cliffs
Engulfing the edifice gradually rock upon rock
Bringing into view greater details and shapes
Clarity
Ever encroaching along the face of the mountain
Causing the shadow to recede
Advancing like an army
Enveloping
Finally coming into full dazzling sunshine!
Every facet visible
In splendor and majesty!
Out of the shadow
Into God's glorious Light!

Did you know?
We were all born in shadow.
Sin being part of our very nature at birth
Ingrained within us, seemingly strong and immoveable
We were hidden away and distant
Living a life apart from God
Until His light shown in our hearts

The light of His salvation!
Breaking forth
God making His presence known in our lives
Ever growing in faith, in the light of Jesus
The Holy Spirit enlightening every area of our being
Illuminating our character and sinful traits
God's Word bringing clarity and understanding
Causing the old life to increasingly recede
Ever guiding us onward
To live a new life that is holy and righteous before God
Causing us to choose to obey His Word
Enveloping our lives with the joy of our salvation
Ever increasing in wonder and praise
As we follow God's leading
Finally causing our lives to be laid bare
Coming before the throne of grace
Where we come face to face with God's glory and majesty
To bask in awe at His amazing grace and love for us
To worship at the feet of Christ, our Lord!
Come out! Come out!
Out of the shadow of sin and doubt
Surrender to the call upon your life!
Repent and be saved!
Live in the Light of Christ forevermore!

Scriptures:

- Genesis 1:3-5 – And God said, "Let there be light," …and he separated the light from the darkness.

- Isaiah 43:18-19 – Forget the former things; do not dwell on the past. See, I am doing a new thing!...

- II Corinthians 4:6 – For God, who said, "Let light shine out of darkness," made his light shine in our hearts to give us the light of the knowledge of the glory of God in the face of Christ.

- II Corinthians 5:17 – Therefore, if anyone is in Christ, he is a new creation; the old has gone, the new has come!
- Colossians 3:1-17 - ...put on the new self, which is being renewed in knowledge in the image of its Creator.
- I Peter 2:9-10 – But you are a chosen people,...that you may declare the praises of him who called you out of darkness into his wonderful light.

Resting in the Light of Christ's love!

God's Dusting

Snowflakes drifting softly downward
      Floating on gusts of clear frigid air
Bits of crystal raindrops in gentle flight
      Wafting in currents without a care
Circling, falling slanted upon the ground
      Flying, swirling sideways without a sound
Covering everything within our sight!
      A winter wonderland of pure delight

Each separate snowflake, unique, never alike
      Puffy, fluffy, like cotton balls of white
Dusting earth's surface with winter charm
      Blanketing roads and highways, houses and farms
Hiding sidewalks and driveways beneath snowy cold
      Capturing trees and fences within its fold
In quiet serenity and peaceful calm
      The Lord's gentle touch upon earth's realm
God's dusting!

God's grace pouring down from the heavenly heights
      More than we can know from our vantage sight
Wondrous grace, above what we can ever know
      The touch of God's gentle hand, His love on us bestowed
Gently cascading to us with forgiveness and love
      From His wondrous throne room high above
Christ's sacrifice made for all of us
      Covering over our unrighteousness

And God blankets us with blessings in our daily lives
      Covering us with joy and peace from realms on high
Hiding us within His protective loving arms

Surrounding and keeping us from earthly harm
Gifting us with family and faithful friends each day
Guiding and leading us lest we would go astray
Touching us by His gentle Spirit as we seek to trust and obey
Looking to see the Lord, face to face, in eternity someday!
God's dusting!

Scriptures:

- Isaiah 1:18-20 - ...though your sins are like scarlet, they shall be as white as snow;...

- Romans 15:13 – May the God of hope fill you with all joy and peace as you trust in him, so that you may overflow with hope by the power of the Holy Spirit.

- Ephesians 1:3-14 – Praise be to the God and Father of our Lord Jesus Christ, who has blessed us in the heavenly realms with every spiritual blessing in Christ.

- Ephesians 2:1-10 - ...But because of his great love for us, God, who is rich in mercy, made us alive with Christ even when we were dead in transgressions—it is by grace you have been saved.

Secure within the palm of God's hand; touched by His grace

"People Watching"

A sunny day at the amusement park
People! They come in all shapes and sizes
People-watching, those waiting in line
Some impatient, others busy talking and laughing
Going from place to place, from ride to ride
Stopping to get an Icee! Eating hot dogs on a stick
Snacking as they go throughout the day
A Texan lady waiting for her grandchildren
With her southern drawl sharing her life, her Christian faith
Another lady with a wide sombrero riding a go-cart
A small child asleep in the side-car
A little boy, walking along, protectively holding his sister's hand
Two small girls with braids, cute as can be
Dancing with glee, smiling and popping their cork poppers
An amusement park employee marching down the street
Being a soldier, in mime, catching the attention of passer-bys
An opinionated older lady sitting in the shade
Telling anyone who will listen that people are way too "fat".
Fathers carrying their children on their shoulders
Mothers keeping a mental track of their family herd
People!
All going their own way; busy having fun
All with their own personality, opinions, thoughts
Their own ideas, agendas
This day…living their life at the amusement park
Going from place to place as they please
A cross-section of society
Some with tunnel vision
Others happy and having a delightful day with family
But with one thing in common
Whether tall, small, skinny or fat

Young, old or middle aged; poor or rich; happy or sad
From different ethnic backgrounds; mixed families
Their common thread!
All needing a Savior!

Does not God above watch the comings and goings of man?
For He reigns over all sovereign and supreme
He sees man's inner being, hears his every thought
Knows intimately his heart desires
Perceives the ways of every individual
Looks upon "his sin" and is grieved
There is no escape!
For all come under the righteous judgment of God!
Oh, how we need a Savior to rescue us from sin and death.
Where can man hide?
For God watches over all!
Turn your eyes toward the One who can save you
Turn your heart toward Christ receiving His salvation
God's mercy and grace to you
Cast your cares upon Him for He loves you!
He is not willing that any should perish.
He desires that you spend eternity with Him.
Abiding in His "watchful" presence!

Scriptures:

- PSALM 33:12-15 – From heaven the LORD looks down and sees all mankind; from his dwelling place he watches all who live on earth…considers everything they do.

- PSALM 121 ALL – …The LORD will keep you from all harm—he will watch over your life; the LORD will watch over your coming and going both now and forevermore.

- JEREMIAH 17:7-10 – "I the LORD search the heart and examine the mind, to reward a man according to his conduct, according

to what his deeds deserve."
- Romans 7:21-25 - …What a wretched man I am! Who will rescue me from this body of death? Thanks be to God—through Jesus Christ our LORD!
- Hebrews 4:14-16 - …let us hold firmly to the faith we profess… let us then approach the throne of grace with confidence so that we may receive mercy and find grace to help us in our time of need.
- Jude 17-25 - …to him who is able to keep you from falling and to present you before his glorious presence without fault and with great joy—to the only God our Savior be glory, majesty, power and authority through Jesus Christ our Lord, before all ages, now and forevermore! Amen.

Thank you LORD for your mercy and grace to me!

Glorious Liberty

Patriotism unfurled and on display!
A lasting symbol of a nation
The American flag flying high!
Arrayed in glorious colors of red, white and blue
The red, a depiction of the cost of priceless freedom
Shed blood of many lives spilled for our liberty
The white standing for the purity of peace
Offered freely to all countrymen
Deepest blue for sparkling skies overhead
The dignity and sanctity of the life of each citizen
And the stars representative of every state in the union
All combined into one nation indivisible
The flag of a nation brilliantly on display
Flying with honor and distinction
Waving in gentle folds upon the breeze
Lifted high upon flagpoles
Held in the palms of small children at parades
Displayed at the graves of the fallen
The patriots throughout America's history
The American flag, "Old Glory"!
Our symbol of freedom
A representation of Glorious Liberty!

But there is another liberty
That far outweighs our nation's freedom
The liberty that comes from knowing Christ, our glorious Savior!
An indescribable freedom of being a child of the King
Christ Jesus our Lord!
We have been given much but not without cost!
The precious blood of Christ shed for "all" mankind on the Cross
Providing salvation to the lost and comfort to the brokenhearted

Eternal life to all who believe!
This Liberty! This Freedom!
This blessing! A free gift!
Ours for the choosing!
As the flag is a symbol of our nation's freedom
The Cross of Christ
Symbolizes our faith in the Risen Lord
The Old Rugged Cross is beautiful beyond compare
Displayed in churches with honor
Golden and adorned but sometimes stark and bare
The focal point
Drawing our attention to Christ's sacrifice
Also worn on chains as jewelry denoting to whom one belongs
We were bought with a price. We belong to Christ!
Perhaps at the graves of those who have gone before us
A symbol of a life lived for the Lord
A symbol of the eternal life we have in Christ
A reminder of the One who died for all of us!
The Cross!
Oh, the Glorious Liberty we have in Christ!

SCRIPTURES:

- ISAIAH 61 ALL – The Spirit of the Sovereign LORD is on me,… to proclaim freedom for the captives and release from darkness for the prisoners…they will be called oaks of righteousness, a planting of the LORD for the display of his splendor.

- MATTHEW 16:24-28 – Then Jesus said to his disciples, "If anyone would come after me, he must deny himself and take up his cross and follow me.

- ROMANS 6:15-23 - …you have been set free from sin and have become slaves to righteousness.…For the wages of sin is death, but the gift of God is eternal life in Christ Jesus our Lord.

- ROMANS 8:1-4 – Therefore, there is now no condemnation for those who are in Christ Jesus, because through Christ Jesus the law of the Spirit of life set me free from the law of sin and death.

- EPHESIANS 2:1-10 - …For it is by grace you have been saved, through faith—and this not from yourselves, it is the gift of God—not by works, so that no one can boast.

- COLOSSIANS 2:6-15 - …God made you alive with Christ. He forgave us all our sins, having canceled the written code, with its regulations,…he took it away, nailing it to the cross… triumphing over them by the cross.

Thanks be to God for His indescribable gift of salvation!

"Got Sludge?"

The huge tanker truck drove directly ahead in my lane.
Moving on down the highway
Going from place to place picking up their load
On the back of the truck in bold letters
"Got Sludge?"
Can you imagine what that brings to mind?
The contents of that tanker
Sludge: what does that mean?
Unwanted refuse and debris
Oil, grime, a mixture of impurities
Muddy, murky deposits and sediments
An acrid and caustic mixture of chemicals
Liquid trash, sewage, ooze and mire
Yuck!
The discards of manufacturing and living refuse
The undesirable leftovers; the dregs
Taken away and discarded
Reprocessed, refined, filtered and made anew
Perhaps useful once again
Or lost forever! A waste!
Got sludge?
Is not life itself, full of sludge?
The undesirable happenings that we wish had never happened?
Our past filled with sin and regret
A mixture of self-will and disobedience
The pits of despair, muddy and murky choices
Wrong decisions, impure thoughts and actions
Worthless living and going our own way
Sludge! Waste!
Each of us has sludge in our past.
How can we discard this unwanted refuse?

The mire that weighs us down
Holds us within its grip
Preventing us from moving forward in life
Stopping us from living a life of freedom and victory
Got sludge?

God has a solution!
A solution for all the sludge in our life!
Christ Jesus, the One who can save us
The One who rescues us out of the mud and the mire
And sets our feet on solid ground
Cast all your cares upon Him because He cares for you!
Bring the sludge of your life to the cross of Christ
He can erase past transgressions, regret and despair
Removing them as far as the east is from the west
Bringing forgiveness and new life
Refining us and washing us clean
Filtering away all the impurities
Causing us to live in newness of life, pleasing to the Lord
Purifying us and cleansing us from all unrighteousness
Through His sacrificial blood by His mercy and love
We are redeemed!
God changes waste and loss into a life that is beautiful
Recycled and made useful in His hand
Got sludge?
Come to Christ who is able to save you!
To the One who reigns forever at the right hand of God!
To the One who is worthy of all our praise!

Scriptures:

- Psalm 40:1-3 – He lifted me out of the slimy pit, out of the mud and mire; he set my feet on a rock and gave me a firm place to stand.

- Psalm 55:22 – Cast your cares on the Lord and he will sustain you; he will never let the righteous fall.
- Psalm 103 All – v.12 – as far as the east is from the west, so far has he removed our transgressions from us.
- Jeremiah 6:27-30 - ...but the refining goes on in vain; the wicked are not purged out.
- Joel 2:25-27 – I will repay you for the years the locusts have eaten--...then you will know...that I am the Lord your God.
- Malachi 3:2-5 - ...For he will be like a refiner's fire or a launderer's soap.
- I Peter 1:3-9 – In his great mercy he has given us new birth into a living hope through the resurrection of Jesus Christ from the dead,...

So grateful for Christ's saving grace and His refining!

"Flying High"

Sky so blue and clear
Snowy white wings overhead
Squawking sea gulls
Circling round and round
High up in the cloudless sky
Wings spread wide open
Gliding!
Soaring!
A flock of ten or twelve
Lost
Out of place
Not where they should be
Out of their element
Inland, far from the sea and open ocean
An uncommon sight over the land
Yet
Gliding!
Soaring!
Free upon the wind!
Flying high!

Mankind
In an uncommon land
Out of God's element
Straying and wandering from God's course
Going in their own direction
Lost
Circling round and round
Not where they should be
Choosing to live life their way
Disobedient and self directed

Far from God's plan and purpose
Needing direction
Groping and grasping after the air
Disoriented
Lost, so lost!

Yet...**GOD!**
He saves us.
He rescues us out of sin and darkness.
God receives us unto Himself.
From where we are
To where He is
No longer lost
Taken back
Redeemed
Forgiven
Forever His!
With a plan and a purpose in life
On His course
Having an eternal home
Gliding!
Soaring!
On His wings
Free
Loved
In His warm embrace
Flying high!

SCRIPTURES:

- EXODUS 19:4-6 – "...how I carried you on eagles' wings and brought you to myself."

- PSALM 61:1-5 – I long to dwell in your tent forever and take refuge in the shelter of your wings.

- JOHN 14:1-4 – "…I am going there to prepare a place for you. And if I go and prepare a place for you, I will come back and take you to be with me that you also may be where I am."
- JOHN 17:24 – "Father, I want those you have given me to be with me where I am, and to see my glory,…"
- I THESSALONIANS 4:13-18 - …will be caught up together with them in the clouds to meet the Lord in the air…
- REVELATION 21:3-4 - …Now the dwelling of God is with men and he will live with them. They will be his people, and God himself will be with them and be their God…

Carried on the wings of Christ!

Clutter Clean-up

What a mess!
Clutter everywhere
Papers, wrappers, cups and glasses
Plates unwashed
Clothes crumpled in piles
Beds unmade
Bills, magazines and leaflets
Empty cereal boxes
Nasty stuff
Dirt
Pet hair, lint and leaves
Smudges on the windows
Scum in the sink
Gooey grease on the stove
Piles of newspapers
Videos and games scattered about
Disarray and disorganization
Odors
Unhealthy conditions
Living amongst the unlivable
Blinded and unseeing
In need of a clutter clean-up!

What clutters up your life?
The stuff of this world
Preoccupations and habits, schedules and agendas
Material things and earthly pleasures
Where do you need to clean-up?
What is strewn about in disarray?
Disorganized?
Nasty stuff that shouldn't be there, spiritually speaking
A cluttered life of sin and regret
Broken relationships, unhealthy lifestyles
So many things clutter our lives

Causing a rift between our God and us
Sin!
We need a clutter clean-up!

There is only One, Christ Jesus, who can do the job!
His sacrifice for our sin
The only thing that can free us from the sin clutter of our lives
He can cleanse us.
Purifying us by His blood from all unrighteousness
He is sufficient, where we are unable.
He can wash us making us whiter than snow.
He can cover our sin with His righteousness.
He can lead us and direct us in a new path and direction.
Un-cluttering all the stuff that does not belong;
All the stuff that is unpleasing to Him.
He strengthens and enables us
To live pure and holy before Him
He is
The Ultimate
Clutter cleaner-upper!

Scriptures:

- PSALM 51:1-12 - ...wash me, and I will be whiter than snow... Create in me a pure heart, O God,...

- ACTS 14:8-18 - ...We are bringing you good news, telling you to turn from these worthless things to the living God,...

- HEBREWS 9:22 – In fact, the law requires that nearly everything be cleansed with blood, and without the shedding of blood there is no forgiveness.

- HEBREWS 10:19-25 - ...let us draw near to God with a sincere heart in full assurance of faith, having our hearts sprinkled to cleanse us from a guilty conscience and having our bodies washed with pure water.

- I JOHN 2:15-17 - ...For everything in the world—comes not from the Father but from the world.

Let us hold unswervingly to the faith we have in Christ!

Chapter 4
God's Love

JOHN 3:16 – "For God so loved the world that he gave his one and only Son, that whoever believes in him shall not perish but have eternal life."

ROMANS 5:8 – But God demonstrates his own love for us in this: While we were still sinners, Christ died for us.

Preface

Love! What other emotion is better than love? We all desire to be loved. Children seek love from their parents, young adults look for the perfect love-mate and people desire the love of friends and family. But there is a love that far outweighs them all…God's love for us! For God's love goes beyond the merely emotional love that we all feel from time to time. God's love is a fact! God loves the creation He has created and we are part of that creation as humankind. God loves is unconditional for His children without any reservation.

It is such a full and complete love for us that God, out of love for us, sent His one and only Son, Christ to die for us in order that we, His children, might be saved. God desires the best for each one of us and desires to spend eternity with us. The fact that He would allow His precious Son to be crucified so that we might live is the full extension of God's love for us. And…Christ loved us enough to die for each one of us! He loved us so much that He was willing to give up His life in order that we might have salvation and eternal life forever.

Have you ever felt unloved? I'm sure you have had that feeling from time to time in your lifetime. We all "feel" misused, put upon, taken for granted, hated and rejected by others. But the love of God goes beyond feelings…it's a sure thing! God loves us! No matter what comes your way, rest upon the fact that God will always love you. Even if you have walked away from Him, He will always desire that you come back, repenting of your sin…come back to His loving arms of love.

Remember the prodigal son (Luke 15:11-32) who left home to seek his fortune? The father was so willing to receive him back home and rejoice over his return. Why? Because he loved his son! Our heavenly Father loves us in the same manner, no matter what we have done. Come back to the love of the Lord who loves you! He waits to show His love toward you!

And we in turn, because of God's great love for us, are to love one another. May we seek to love our neighbor as we love our self (I Corinthians 13:4-13), expressing the love that God has shown to us.

A Father's Love

He's strong!
He's the one you seek when you're in trouble.
You talk to mom but dad fixes things.
Most times, he's quiet.
But when he speaks, his words are wise.
He works hard.
Diligent, providing for his family
The one you run to at the end of the day when he returns home.
"Daddy, daddy, daddy…daddy's home!"
He has a quiet love expressed in his faithfulness
Shown by his actions and the things he does
He's passionate for sports;
Basketball, golf, hockey, football…cheering for the home team
Loves cars…anything with four-wheels
Enjoys the outdoors
Grows things in the garden with his hands
Gets dirty and sweaty
Repairs anything that's broken
Watches over a sleeping child in the wee hours of the night
Fathers are great!
An example of our heavenly Father above
Demonstrating a love that's unconditional and unchanging
A love that transcends time and space
A love that keeps on loving
Willing to sacrifice anything
No matter what!

"Abba, Father"!
How strong and unchanging You are.
The One to whom we can come, with any trouble or woe
The One who hears and intently listens

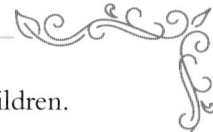

The One who cares about us and loves us, His children.
How gracious You are.
Forgiving us when we falter
Setting us upon a Rock and helping us to stand firm
Teaching us Your ways
Causing us to live righteous before You
Watching over us
Looking upon us with eyes of love
Having understanding and compassion
Faithful…always faithful!
Dependable…providing for our every need
Expressing love beyond measure
Sending Jesus, Your Son to save us
Redeeming us when we were unlovable and lost
Mighty and majestic…high and lifted up!
Creator and Ruler over all!
King of kings and Lord of lords!
Supreme, the Lord Almighty!
"Abba, Father"
How awesome You are!
We don't deserve your abundant love.
Oft-times we go astray but thank you for loving us!
How wonderful You are in all the earth!

Scriptures:

- DEUTERONOMY 7:7-9 - …Know therefore, that the LORD your God is God; he is the faithful God, keeping his covenant of love to a thousand generations of those who love him and keep his commands.

- PSALM 86 ALL – v.5 – You are forgiving and good, O LORD, abounding in love to all who call to you.

- JOHN 1:12-13 – Yet to all who believed him, to those who believed in his name, he gave the right to become children of God.

- ROMANS 8:14-17 - ...And by him (the Spirit) we cry, "Abba, Father." ...we are God's children.
- EPHESIANS 6:1-4 - ...Fathers, do not exasperate your children; instead, bring them up in the training and instruction of the Lord.
- I JOHN 3:1-3 – How great is the love the Father has lavished on us, that we should be called children of God!

Blessed to be God's child and loved by Him!

Lasting Love

The gentle mourning doves are mating!
Small brownish birds of the pigeon family
Flying in gliding swoops from tree to tree
Busy in their playful banter
Cooing in soft tones of contentment with a sad melancholy call
Their tone more adamant during their courting ritual
With sharp squawking sounds
Displaying a "coyness" between the mating pair
Almost hopping with glee up and down above the ground
A fluffing of fluttering feathers
Wings outstretched toward their intended mate
A dance of love
They say that mourning doves bond for life!
Deeply affectionate to their mate
Displaying the essence of human togetherness
"A once and always" kind of love
Enduring to the end "'til death us do part"
In faithfulness to one another
In love, a lasting love!

For love is a choice!
Just as we choose a mate to have and to hold
God in love chose us!
Even when we were opposed to Him and heaped in sin
For God's love far exceeds our imaginings or understanding!
Because God's love is unconditional
Not dependent upon whom we are or what we do
God's love is unmerited, a free gift.
Even when we are prideful and self righteous
Loving us even when we don't deserve it
God's love is gentle and tender.

Even when we are hard, overbearing and cruel
God's love is a patient love.
Even when we are impatiently in a hurry and cannot wait
Even when we don't take the time to be alone with Him
God's love is unfailing.
Even when we fail to seek Him, time and time again
God's love is an enduring love.
He remembers us and keeps on loving us.
Even when we wander down a different path forgetting Him
God's love is a forgiving love.
Even when we are unforgiving to others
Even when we can't forgive ourselves
God's love beckons us to His side.
Drawing us, wooing us
Even when we desire to go in the opposite direction
God's love is a sacrificial love.
It is a love that sacrificed God's only begotten Son on our behalf.
Christ died in our place, enduring to the end.
Because of His great love for us!
God's love is limitless and unending.
We cannot run out of the love that God has for us!
God's love is everlasting!
Desiring us to spend eternity in His majestic presence!
Are you in love with Him?

SCRIPTURES:

- PSALM 36:5-10 – Your love, O LORD, reaches to the heavens, your faithfulness to the skies.

- PSALM 51:1-12 – Have mercy on me, O God, according to your unfailing love; according to your great compassion…

- JOHN 6:35-51 – Then Jesus declared, "I am the bread of life. … No one can come to me unless the Father who sent me draws him, and I will raise him up at the last day."

- Romans 5:8 – But God demonstrates his own love for us in this: While we were still sinners, Christ died for us.

- I Corinthians 13:1-13 - …Love never fails. …And now these three remain: faith, hope and love. But the greatest of these is love.

- Ephesians 3:14-21 - …And I pray that you, being rooted and established in love, may have power, together with all the saints, to grasp how wide and long and high and deep is the love of Christ, and to know this love that surpasses knowledge—that you may be filled to the measure of all the fullness of God.

- I John 4:7-21 - …God is love. …This is love: not that we loved God, but that he loved us and sent his Son as an atoning sacrifice for our sins. …We love because he first loved us.

Thank you Lord for the love that You have for me!

A Strand of Pearls

They are radiantly beautiful!
A strand of luxurious, perfectly round pearls
Soft and smooth
Given long ago by a loving grandfather
They have a glow about them.
A luster!
Strung in a row from largest to smallest
Each gently touching the one adjacent
Worn through the years with honor and loving memories
Precious!
Never going out of fashion! Timeless!
Yet considered "old fashioned" by some
None the less, having an elegance all their own
Held together by a tiny silver clasp
But
If broken
Pearls would scatter in all directions
Lost under furniture, rolling along the floor
Oh, to find them all!
Not to lose one!
The treasured and cherished
Strand of pearls!
Oh, that we would look with the same eyes
Upon our life "in Christ"!
Like a strand of pearls
A life given to us by a loving Father
A God who loves us!
Desiring that our life reflect Him in every way
Bringing Him glory and praise
For we wear His robe of righteousness all day long
And our life is held together

By the clasp of His unending love
Cherished and treasured
We are encircled by His tender care and mercy
And yet…
Without God in our life…
We would be scattered in all directions
Lost!
Unstrung, worthless, unusable
For Christ is the One who holds us secure
For He never goes out of fashion
He is our Redeemer, the Savior of our soul.
He brings purpose and a plan to our life
A reason for living!
For we are bound to Him and by Him
He is our pearl of great price!
Our treasure and great reward!
Precious in every way!
Exceedingly great!
Far above…a strand of pearls!

Scriptures:

- MATTHEW 13:44-46 - …the kingdom of heaven is like a merchant looking for fine pearls. When he found one of great value, he went away and sold everything he had and bought it.
- I JOHN 4:7-12 - …This is love: not that we loved God, but that he loved us and sent his Son as an atoning sacrifice for our sins.
- REVELATION 21:21 - The twelve gates were twelve pearls, each gate made of a single pearl. The great street of the city was of pure gold, like transparent glass.

How precious is Christ, our Lord!
Thank you, that I am your treasured possession!

Ice Cream with K.J.!

The perfect day!
Time together!
Let's have some ice cream, K.J.!
A 3 year olds delight.
Oh, the choices!
Oreo mint, chocolate, bubble gum, vanilla
A difficult choice to decide
With ice cream in hand, finding a booth and scooting in!
Talking, laughing, sharing a moment in time
With occasional ice cream drips
Napkins at the ready!
Enjoying the icy treats
Tasting each other's flavors
Mmmmm!
They are all so good!
Sharing and interchanging each other's ice cream
As if it was our own
Piling the bubble gum balls on a napkin for later chewing
Perfect oneness!
Sublime joy and laughter
Ice cream completely consumed with satisfaction
God's momentary gift of love shared!

Oh, that we could always share this kind of communion
With our heavenly Father!
A oneness of spirit
Time in hallowed togetherness
Delighting in His fellowship
Choosing to be with Him
Enjoying His presence
All of who He truly is

Sharing moments of our time to commune with Him in prayer
Tasting and seeing
That He is good!
Interchanging our sinfulness for His love and grace
Sharing with others the truth of His Word
Giving His peace and love
To those whom we have opportunity
Piling the gifts of His Spirit ever more firmly into our lives
Finding joy and laughter
Complete elation and satisfaction in God, Himself
A perfect oneness!
With the One who loves us unconditionally!
Who desires to share our moments, our very lives
Do you not desire to share your time with Him?

Scriptures:

- PSALM 34:8 – Taste and see that the Lord is good;

- JOHN 15:1-17 - Remain in my love…so that my joy may be in you and that your joy may be complete.

- I TIMOTHY 6:17-19 - …but put their hope in God, who richly provides us with everything for our enjoyment.

- I JOHN 1 ALL - …And our fellowship is with the Father and with his Son, Jesus Christ.

Thank you Lord for the loving moments you give to us!

God's Promises

Wow!
There it is before our earthly eyes
Seemingly coming out of nowhere
Traveling on the crisp after-rain mist
Shining through the sunlight
Back-dropped by majestic snowy mountains
Sparkling in subtle hues of vibrant colors
Ultraviolet, blues and greens
Fading to golden yellow and rosy red
A RAINBOW!
Arched across the late afternoon sky
Gorgeous! Glorious!
Of pure delight!
God's demonstration of His unimaginable glory
His promise to the world in Noah's day,
An everlasting promise
To never flood the earth in such a way again
Remaining a sign to us in our day
Of God's faithfulness and love
Filled with hope
Bearing His Sovereignty over the earth
To our day and future generations
A fulfillment of His will
God's Promises!

For His Promises are…
…true to His faithfulness to keep them.
…dependent upon His Sovereignty
…in line with His plan and purpose
…graced upon us by His love
…sure because He always keeps His Word

...trustworthy for God does not lie
...good, pure and holy, because that is part of God's attributes
...unbelievable but God can do all things
...eternal because God in unchanging

What promises has God given unto you?
First and foremost, the promise of His only begotten Son
Jesus Christ, Our Living Lord!
And
Because of Jesus in our lives,
The promise of...
...cleansing from all unrighteousness, the forgiveness of sin
...His presence to all who believe
...being sealed by His Holy Spirit for eternity
...knowing Him through His Holy Word, the Bible
...talents and gifts to be used for His glory
...hardship and suffering, in order to mold and shape us unto maturity
...a place in the Lamb's book of life
...an eternal heavenly home
And
So much more in abundance
Blessing upon blessing!
God's Promises!

Will you not thank Him with your worship and praise?

SCRIPTURES:

- NUMBERS 23:19 – God is not a man, that he should lie, nor a son of man, that he should change his mind. Does he speak and then not act? Does he promise and not fulfill?

- PSALM 145 ALL – ...The LORD is faithful to all his promises and loving toward all he has made.

- JOHN 3:16 – "For God so loved the world that he gave his one and only Son, that whoever believes in him shall not perish but have eternal life."

- ROMANS 4:16-25 - ...being fully persuaded that God had power to do what he had promised.
- EPHESIANS 1:3-14 – Praise be to the God and Father of our Lord Jesus Christ, who has blessed us in the heavenly realms with every spiritual blessing in Christ.
- HEBREWS 10:23 – Let us hold unswervingly to the hope we profess, for he who promised is faithful.
- I JOHN 2:24-25 - ...this is what he promised us—even eternal life.

Holding on to God's promises and giving thanks

The Perfect Pumpkin

The pumpkin patch in fall!
Somewhat obscured and hidden within a shaded glen
Surrounded by fruit trees of oranges and persimmons
Down a straw-strewn pathway
With old fashioned lampposts and twinkling lights
With tractors and hay rides
Farm animals
Baaing sheep and squiggly pigs
All part of the wonderful fall season
And pumpkins!
Rows and rows of pumpkins
Scattered amid the hay bales
Stacked side-by-side covering the ground
Big giant ones, small tiny ones
Odd shaped with defects and creases
Mostly brilliant orange
But also gray ones, rosy ones, white ones
A landscape of circular color and design
All wanting to be taken home to be enjoyed
To become pumpkin pie and yummy treats
Jack-o-lanterns
Or just merely decorations on the kitchen table
Oh, to find the perfect pumpkin!

Choices!
Does God not choose us, before we chose Him?
Does He not call us out of darkness?
Into His Glorious light!
How different we all are.
Each person unique, each gifted in varied ways
With different talents and traits

As varied as the pumpkins
Some short, some tall, some round, some thin
Long hair, short hair, no hair
Looking differently with unique characteristics
Yet God calls us to come!
To be part of His family
Using each one of us for His glory
To serve Him because He is worthy
Has not God loved us with an everlasting love?
Sacrificing Christ his own Son
So that we might live
Desiring to have a relationship with us
No matter whom we are or what we have done
Forgiving us unconditionally to be His very own child
God has a plan and a purpose for each and every life
For we are useable in His hands
Made holy, righteous and acceptable
Perfected in God's sight!
Through the cleansing blood of Christ
Perfect in every way!
To the praise of His Glory!

Will you not chose Him?
For He desires you!

Scriptures:

- **Psalm 18:30-36** —As for God, his way is perfect;…It is God who arms me with strength and makes my way perfect.

- **John 15:16** – You did not choose me, but I chose you and appointed you to go and bear fruit—fruit that will last.

- **Ephesians 1:3-14** - …for he chose us in him before the creation of the world to be holy and blameless in his sight. In love he predestined us to be adopted as his sons through Jesus

Christ, in accordance with his pleasure and will—to the praise of his glorious grace, which he has freely given us in the One he loves.

- I Peter 2:9-10 —But you are a chosen people, a royal priesthood, a holy nation, a people belonging to God, that you may declare the praises of him who called you out of darkness into his wonderful light. …but now you are the people of God;

Praising God for his love for me

DISCIPLINED

"No, No, No!"
Screaming, hollering, with kicking of feet
"Are you going to do what I told you?"
"No!"
"Sit in time out if you will not obey."
"No!"
"Are you going to listen to what I said?"
"No!"
Picked up…put in time out.
Screaming, hollering, with more kicking of feet
"Are you going to do what I told you?"
"No, No, No!"
"You will sit in time out until you will."
Screaming, hollering and still kicking of feet
Wooden spoon!
Crying, screaming, hollering, kicking with vigor
"Will you do what I told you to do?"
Whimpering!
"Will you do what I told you to do?"
Crying, gasping for air
Softly…with tears, "Yes, Mommy"
Loving, holding, drawing close within mothers loving arms
"I love you."
"Let's go do what I told you to do."
"Okay Mom!"

Are we not like small children sometimes?
"No, No, No!"
Not a small child's response but a grown adult.
Screaming at life hollering against the world
Kicking against the Lord's instruction

"Are you going to do what I have told you in my Word?"
"No!"
Sit in God's time out away from His presence
Grieving the Holy Spirit
Angry and mad
Stubborn, continuing to go in your own direction
"Are you going to do what I have told you in my Word?"
God's Spirit speaks gently yet firmly.
"Are you listening?" "Are you willing to comply?"
"Maybe!"
"Is discipline necessary?"
"I can do things my way without your help."
Consequences of hardship, suffering and pain
At the end of your rope
"Are you going to obey?"
"Yes, Lord." "There is no One like you!"
"Forgive me."
"I am ready to listen and obey."
"Show me what you would have me to do."
"Lead me in the way everlasting."
"Guide me by your Word."
Gently held and caressed within His loving arms
Forgiven and loved
Protected
Saved by His grace and loved unconditionally.
"Abba Father"
"Show me Your ways."
"Help me to obey!"

Scriptures:

- Job 5:17 – Blessed is the man whom God corrects; so do not despise the discipline of the Almighty.

- Proverbs 13:24 – He who spares the rod hates his son, but he who loves him is careful to discipline him.

- JOHN 14:21 – Whoever has my commands and obeys them, he is the one who loves me…
- ROMANS 8:15-17 - …and by him we cry, "Abba, Father." …we are God's children.
- I CORINTHIANS 11:32 – When we are judged by the Lord, we are being disciplined so that we will not be condemned with the world.
- HEBREWS 12:1-12 - … "My son, do not make light of the Lord's discipline,…the Lord disciplines those he loves,…"

Seeking to obey in response to God's love for me

Summer Rain

It comes so unexpectedly
Clouds darken the sky, blotting out the sun.
One drop, then another
Slowly
Out of the heavens above
Refreshing
Filling the air with a sweet aroma
Cooling the atmosphere
Gaining momentum
Thunder sounds in the distance
Raindrops washing off plants and trees
Bringing much needed water
The pitter-patter upon the rooftop
Running off and filling the gutters.
Puddles appearing on the cement
Droplets making circlets upon the surface
Causing the cat to seek refuge
Yet hummingbirds remain unhindered in flight
Still feeding at their feeder
A respite from the heat of summer
A blessing from the hand of God
Touching the earth below
And then it's gone!
The storm is over.
But, oh the wonder of a summer rain!

God's blessings
Sometimes so unexpected
In the midst of trials and hard times
His grace and love extended
To a dry and thirsty land
The sun and moon to shine
A wonderful summer rain

Given to all of us
Freely, without cost
Life and breath
Family and friends
His glorious creation
Filling us up to overflowing
Our hearts cannot contain
All the blessings our gracious Lord has given,
Falling like showers into our lives.
His mercy and forgiveness
Washing us clean
Restoring our relationship with Him
Causing us to walk in His presence
How wonderful Christ's love is for us!

Lord, cause us to be truly grateful.
For all that You continually bestow upon us
Your wonderful daily rain!
Raining down on us!

Scriptures:

- **Deuteronomy 7:9, 13** – Know therefore that the LORD your God is God; he is the faithful God,…He will love you and bless you…

- **Psalm 93 All** – The LORD reigns, he is robed in majesty,… mightier than the thunder of the great waters,…the LORD on high is mighty.

- **Ezekiel 34:23-31** – "…there will be showers of blessing. …I am your God, declares the Sovereign LORD."

- **Matthew 5:45** – …and sends rain on the righteous and the unrighteous.

- **Ephesians 1:3-14** – Spiritual Blessings in Christ

Enjoying the summer rain, washed in God's love

Enveloped in Love

What a beautiful sight while the stars are still so bright
The crystal moon shines so clearly overhead, so well defined
Surrounded, enveloped, encircled with light
A glowing halo around the moon in the night sky
Such a sparkling halo is such a rare and beautiful sight
That spacious circle of light shining in the night's darkness
Refractions of light bouncing off tiny ice particles
The atmosphere filled with God's wondrous greatness
This encircling halo in the expansive heavens high above
Is such a wondrous expression of our Father's gracious love!

For God's love is…
    …unconditional,
        We can't earn it, it's a gift.
    …complete and full, enormous,
        Shown by all that He does for us daily
    …sacrificial, freely given,
        Christ died to set us free.
    …protective and always caring,
        His child and friend we'll always be.
    …so unfailing and dependable,
        No matter what comes our way.
    …never-ending, He won't leave us,
        It's constant and unchanging, every day.

Can you not help to imagine, God's wondrous love for you?
How you are enveloped forever in His loving arms so true?
His light shines softly, caressing your gentle face,
You are held close within His grasp, in His warm embrace.
God daily encircles and envelops you in His gracious, caring love,
One day, you'll be with Him, face to face,
    In His heavenly realm above!

Scriptures:

- DEUTERONOMY 7:9 – Know therefore that the LORD your God is God; he is the faithful God, keeping his covenant of love to a thousand generations of those who love him and keep his commands.
- PSALM 31 All –v.7 I will be glad and rejoice in your love,…
- JOHN 3:16 – "For God so loved the world that he gave his one and only Son, that whoever believes in him shall not perish but have eternal life.
- ROMANS 5:8 – But God demonstrates his own love for us in this: While we were still sinners, Christ died for us.
- I CORINTHIANS 13:4-13 – Love is patient, love is kind…It always protects, always trusts, always hopes, always perseveres. Love never fails….

Enveloped in His Love

Two Pink Roses

They were two perfect buds
Growing stately atop long slender stems
Palest pink, soft and delicate
Ready to burst forth in blossom
Glowing in the afternoon sunshine
In the distance, two little girls came into view
Riding their scooters along the sidewalk
Stopping to chat with beaming smiles on their faces
Chatter-boxes talking about everything at once
Momentarily distracted, admiring the perfect roses
With longing eyes, drawn to their beauty
Not asking for anything
Given!
Surrendered freely to two tiny cheerful hearts
With scissors, the roses are cut to length
Thorns removed with care
Purple chrysanthemums added in the tiny bouquet
Crimson ribbon cut and tied securely in a bow
The blossoms placed in the outstretched hands of each little girl
Taken and shared with both of their mothers at home
Bringing joy to another's heart
Two pink roses!
Has not God blessed us to be a blessing?
To share what has been given
To love as He would have us to love
To be a witness to the great gift He has bestowed to us
The gift of life in Christ our Lord!
For He is our precious Rose of Sharon!
Beautiful! Perfect and unblemished!
Yet there was no beauty that drew all men to Himself
Glowing in majesty and grace

Our perfect Lamb of God!
That takes away the sin of the world
Given by a loving Heavenly Father
His only begotten Son surrendered unto death
Death on the Cross
Given for us, His lost children
Cut down in the prime of life
Wearing a crown of thorns
Tied securely, bound
Placed upon the barren wooden Cross
Bearing our shame and reproach
And yet…the joy that was set before Him
Because of His great love for us!
How can we not love in return?
How can we withhold "anything" from our precious Lord?
Not even…two pink roses!

Scriptures:

- JOHN 1:29-34 - … "Look, the Lamb of God, who takes away the sin of the world!"

- HEBREWS 12:2 – Let us fix our eyes on Jesus, the author and perfecter of our faith, who for the joy set before him endured the cross, scorning its shame, and sat down at the right hand of the throne of God.

- I JOHN 4:7-21 - …This is love: not that we loved God, but that he loved us and sent his Son as an atoning sacrifice for our sins. Dear friends, since God so loved us, we also ought to love one another.

Desiring to surrender all because of God's great love for me!

Beyond "ken"!

Webster's Dictionary – ken (noun) – range of vision, sight, view, range of perception, understanding, or knowledge

It was truly a surprise! So unexpected!
A birthday like no other!
To think that all these people were here to celebrate "me"!
Beyond words to express my amazement
Friends from days gone by
New friends joining the group
Neighbors from across the street
Cherished Bible study gals
Family all here with cheerful faces
Even coming from across the miles to attend
And all the grandchildren
Some fully grown, some still growing
And little guys with eager eyes and energy
They have all come!
Bearing gifts and congratulations!
Good wishes and fond memories
Expressing extra-ordinary love with generous hearts
Amazing! Beyond understanding and imagining!
Feeling totally undeserving, unworthy of so much attention
Beyond "ken"!

But…isn't that the same as we feel before God?
Unworthy and undeserving of His love
And fully amazed that He would love us anyway
Unconditionally and in spite of ourselves
Loving us totally and completely
Just as we are!
Forgiving us beyond measure

Erasing our sin and shame
Restoring us in righteousness before Him
Lavishing upon us His many blessings
Gracing us daily with undeserved favor
Now and in the heavenly realms
Bestowing upon us His Holy Spirit
Nurturing us and growing us into a person of worth
A person pleasing to the Lord
Surrounding us with His very presence
As we seek Him in prayer
It is so beyond our understanding!
Hard to imagine that God would desire to do all this
For us!
And yet we are so glad that He has taken us as His own.
His love for us is beyond measure
For He has sent His only Son, Christ, to die in our place
To redeem us and make us a child of the King!
God's unfailing love for the lost!
And His faithfulness to all generations!
There is rejoicing in heaven when a lost soul comes to Him
Joy forevermore!
Unfathomable!
Far beyond "ken"!

Oh, that we would seek to praise God's Holy name!

SCRIPTURES:

- PSALM 33:18-22 - ...May your unfailing love rest upon us, O LORD, even as we put our hope in you.

- PSALM 36:5-10 – Your love, O LORD, reaches to the heavens, your faithfulness to the skies.

- ISAIAH 40:28 – The LORD is the everlasting God, the Creator of the end of the earth...and his understanding no one can fathom.

- JEREMIAH 31:3 - ..."I have loved you with an everlasting love; I have drawn you with lovingkindness.
- I PETER 1:3-9 - ...Though you have not seen him, you love him;...and are filled with an inexpressible and glorious joy, for you are receiving the goal of your faith, the salvation of your souls.
- I JOHN 4:7-21 - ...This is love: not that we loved God, but that he loved us and sent his Son as an atoning sacrifice for our sins. ...We love because he first loved us.

Rejoicing over the inexpressible love God has shown to me!

In Loving Closeness

I hear his footfall upon the stairs
Coming downstairs from his naptime
He rounds the corner with sleep still in his eyes
A slight grin on his face as he comes into my sight
Grandchildren are a special gift from God
Bringing back memories of children, now grown
He hops onto the couch, coming near
Happy to see me
He comes to snuggle in the crook of my arm
His hair tousled and still damp from sleeping
Having that "smell" of youth
Snuggly soft and touchable
We just sit together for a time
"Mister Jabber-box"
Talking about everything and nothing
"How did your day go?"
"Did you have fun at your friend's house?"
"Are you ready for Easter?"
Just an intimate time together
Nothing special and yet, worth everything!
In loving closeness!

Such a reminder of our heavenly Father
In loving closeness to us!
Where can you go that God is not there?
You can hear Him in the rustling of the leaves
In the quiet of darkest night
He is around every corner and also by your side
There is nowhere that He is out of sight
He is as close as a breath and as far as eternity!
God is limitless!

Beyond our comprehending
And yet…He longs for us, His children!
He wants us to come to Him and seek His face
To snuggle within His arms of love
To call Him, our "Abba Father"!
Oh, how He longs for an intimate relationship with us!
To have a personal "one on one" with us!
To talk about all the things on our mind
Everything and the tiniest nothings of life
To guide us in the way we should go
To teach us and lead us in the paths of righteousness
Forgiving all our past failures and sin
Time together with our heavenly Father
Oh, so very special!
Worth everything!
Coming near
For we indeed have access to God Himself
For Jesus has made a way for us
Behind the curtain into the Most Holy Place
Before the throne of God Almighty!
Won't you come?
Won't you spend some time with the Father?
Within His loving arms
Basking in the light of God's Word and in deep prayer
Desiring to know Him better
In loving closeness!

Scriptures:

- Psalm 34:18 – The LORD is close to the brokenhearted and saves those who are crushed in spirit.

- Psalm 73:28 – But as for me, it is good to be near God. I have made the Sovereign LORD my refuge; I will tell of all your deeds.

- Psalm 105:1-4 - …Look to the LORD and his strength; seek his face always.
- Matthew 11:28-30 – "Come to me, all you who are weary and burdened, and I will give you rest…
- Romans 8:15-17 - …but you received the Spirit of sonship. And by him we cry, "Abba, Father." The Spirit himself testifies with our spirit that we are God's children. …heirs of God and co-heirs with Christ,…
- Hebrews 10:19-25 – v. 22 - …let us draw near to God with a sincere heart in full assurance of faith
- I John 3:1-3 – How great is the love the Father has lavished on us, that we should be called children of God! And that is what we are!

So blessed knowing that I am a child of God!

Love's Kiss

Gentleness in liquid form
Escaping from the misty clouds overhead
Rain slowly falling earthward
Not in heavy torrents
But
Softly, silently
The calm pitter-patter on rooftops and sidewalks
Causing us to stop and listen
To enjoy
Ringlets of circles upon standing puddles
Refreshment to thirsty plants and trees
Soaking and saturating the dry ground
Washing leaves and petals rinsing away dust and grime
Bringing life
Clear sparkling raindrops reviving heart and soul
A soothing balm from heaven's door
God's cleansing touch
A delicate washing of His creation
A quiet passing rain
A subtle connection between earth and sky
God bending low making His presence known
Touching the earth
Love's kiss!

Oh Lord, that You would touch our lives today!
Making Your presence known anew!
In gentleness, softly speaking words of love and peace
Silently whispering through your Holy Spirit into our ears
Causing us to stop and listen
To hear and respond to Your beckoning call
To let Your Holy Word

Refresh and saturate our thirsty and barren hearts
Soothing us with Your words of hope and love
Your peace unending
Allowing Your life to restore us
Reviving our hearts and soul once again
Causing us to live in newness of life
Cleansing us with Your forgiveness and peace
By the transforming blood of Christ, our Lord
Who by His grace
Allows us access to God's heavenly throne room
Before our Mighty King!

How great is the love that the Father has lavished on us!
His love is ever patient and kind
His love never fails
All things may pass away
But His love remains constant and unchanging
He loves us with a never-ending love
Gently like a raindrop falling upon our cheek
In tenderness
God bending low making His presence known
Touching our lives
Love's kiss!

That we would choose to love as He has loved us!
Our love kiss to others!

SCRIPTURES:

- PSALM 36:5-10 – Your love, O LORD, reaches to the heavens, your faithfulness to the skies,...

- JEREMIAH 31:3 – ... "I have loved you with an everlasting love; I have drawn you with loving-kindness."

- JOHN 3:16 – For God so loved the world that he gave his one and only Son, that whoever believes in him shall not perish but have eternal life.

- ROMANS 5:8 – But God demonstrates his own love for us in this: While we were still sinners, Christ died for us.
- I CORINTHIANS 13 ALL – Love is patient, love is kind. Love never fails.
- EPHESIANS 3:14-19 - ...so that Christ may dwell in your hearts through faith...to grasp how wide and long and high and deep is the love of Christ, and to know this love that surpasses knowledge—that you may be filled to the measure of all the fullness of God.
- I JOHN 4:7-21 – GOD IS LOVE. ...We love because he first loved us.

Resting in the love of Christ!

Chapter 5
God's Creation

GENESIS 1:1 – In the beginning God created the heavens and the earth.

COLOSSIANS 1:15-16 – He is the image of the invisible God, the firstborn over all creation. For by him all things were created: things in heaven and on earth, visible and invisible, whether thrones or powers or rulers or authorities; all things were created by him and for him

Preface

Isn't God's Creation wonderful! Have you ever sat on the beach and watched the waves break upon the shore or seen the marvelous colors upon the water and sky as the sun slips beneath the horizon? Or…have you looked upon the mountains and seen their majestic peaks, their grandeur before your eyes? Perhaps you have gazed upon a hummingbird in flight and were astounded by their gorgeous coloring. All these and so much more are part of God's wondrous Creation, His handiwork.

Do you believe that God created it? For in the beginning, God created the heavens and the earth (Genesis 1). Do you believe that fact? God created the Garden of Eden for the first human beings, Adam and Eve. Everything was perfect until they disobeyed God and were cast out of the garden. The world that we see today has been corrupted by sin and death. We see a polluted version of the creation that God made in the beginning and yet our world still reveals the intended beauty of its Creator. Our world and the universe are a reflection of a most wondrous and glorious God. How can we not praise and thank Him for all that He has created and provided for us?

And yet in our world there are naturalist, evolutionists and people who take God's creation for granted and ignore the One who so meticulously and lovingly created our universe for our enjoyment. I met a young fellow on an airplane one time who was such a person. He was a mountain climber who had traversed the globe climbing mountain peaks throughout the world. He marveled at the majesty that surrounded him on his climbing treks…but he never praised God for the wonder that was before his eyes. How sad to see God's creation and not praise the Maker of it all.

And did you know…God is planning for a new Creation?

A new heaven and a new earth! And a Holy City, the new Jerusalem where God himself will dwell with men and be their God (Revelation 21:1-8). An exciting future awaits all of God's people…for God is the Alpha and Omega, Creator of all things!

DUSK

Dusk!
Wherein lays the sanctuary of the Lord!
Look up and see!
God painting dramatic colors across the heavens
Spanning horizon to horizon, a vibrant landscape
Wispy clouds catching every hue
The vanishing sun setting them ablaze in reds and oranges
Fading to soft subtle pinks and purples
Coloring the blue of advancing nighttime
Hush and be still!
The late afternoon breeze has quieted
Gentle stillness blankets the evening sky
Trees stop their swaying
A few black crows squawk across the sky's expanse
Echoing into the distance
But all is hushed.
Come and see the greatness of the Lord!
Displayed in majesty before our eyes
Stop!
View the splendor of His wondrous creation
In awe and reverence
Laid out before us in all its glory!
Dusk!

Does not God call us?
Even in the quietness of dusk?
In the stillness of a sunset
Calling our name
Seeking our presence
In the sanctuary of the Almighty
To come!
"Seek my face," says the Lord
"Seek Me, while I may be found."

The day stretches forth into night.
Come and fellowship with Me.
Spend a quiet moment in My presence
At the feet of Jesus
Touching the hem of His garment
In reverence and awe
Spending time in sweet communion
Hallowing His name
Holy! Holy! Holy!
Praise be to the Sovereign God!
Who reigns supreme in glory!

Will you come?
Dusk is advancing.
Come and worship!
Night draws nigh!
The Day of the LORD approaches
Like a thief in the night
Come!

Scriptures:

- I Chronicles 16:23-36 - Sing to the LORD, all the earth; proclaim his salvation day after day, …For great is the LORD and most worthy of praise…ascribe to the LORD the glory due his name.

- Psalm 19:1-6 – The heavens declare the glory of God; the skies proclaim the work of his hands.

- Psalm 150 – Praise the LORD. Praise God in his sanctuary; praise him in his mighty heavens. Praise him for his acts of power; praise him for his surpassing greatness. … Let everything that has breath praise the LORD. Praise the LORD.

- Colossians 1:15-20 – He is the image of the invisible God, the firstborn over all creation. For by him all things were created.

With praise to my Lord for His wondrous creation!

God in the Details

Autumn's glorious season,
> Displaying God's wondrous grace

The brilliance of the falling leaves
> Raining upon the scenic landscape

Gently changing from summer's warmth
> To cooler, crisp days of fall

Filled with stunning splendor
> For observant eyes to behold

Leaves cascading downward
> Gently slipping to the ground

In unnoticed quiet silence
> Making barely a single sound

Blanketing the ground, crunching beneath our feet
> Piling in gentle mounds in yards, along most every street

Colors in reddish yellow, orange and golden hues,
> Painting the autumn landscape, making a splendid view

But take notice of the details
> Of each and every leaf

So intricate and delicate
> With veins of color beyond belief

No single leaf exactly
> The same as any other

None alike and uniquely different
> From its adjacent brother

Made in God's perfection,
> Changing color at the proper time

So wondrous in their pattern,
> Supremely glorious and sublime

All placed within God's plan and purpose
> Within His grand design

Here for just a season
> Quickly gone, swiftly passing into time

Every leaf, a part of God's creation from when time first began
> Every detail, shape and color held within His hand

And yet, of God's wondrous creation
> Made with perfection and lovingly for us

He considers man His valued treasure
> Every detail of our lives to Him so very precious

Each facet of our days is held within His tender care
> Totally known by Him and perfect beyond compare

Are we not more loved than all the glorious leaves?
> Aren't we blessed abundantly by what we have received?

Should we not be thankful for each and every day?
> For God is in the details as we go along our way

Let us then with prayerful hearts thank our Father up above
> for His tender mercy, grace, and abiding love.

Let us come before our most Sovereign Lord
> And kneel humbly before His glorious throne

And worship Him and exalt His name
> For He reigns and rules forevermore!

Psalm 100

Shout for joy to the LORD, all the earth. Worship the LORD with gladness; come before him with joyful songs.

Know that the LORD is God. It is he who made us, and we are his; we are his people, the sheep of his pasture.

Enter his gates with thanksgiving and his courts with praise; give thanks to him and praise his name.

For the LORD is good and his love endures forever; his faithfulness continues through all generations.

Thankful that the Lord is concerned with the details of my life

Unfettered Worship

They rise early
Their lyrical song drifting on the cool morning air
Melodious, unfettered
Who can stop their joyful awakening?
Proclaiming the dawning to a new day
Bringing music to the heart and soul
Songbirds in worship
Singing praises to the Lord above
Likewise
All nature joins in harmony together
The mountains declare the majesty of the Lord
The flowers sing forth the aroma of God's undying sweet love
The heavens awake to declare His greatness
Crying forth, shouting His praise
Calling our eyes skyward
To our glorious Lord reigning in the heavenly realms
The rocks and the trees whisper in chorus
How great thou art, O Lord!
Bringing forth praise
In unfettered worship!

Arise!
Now is the time to worship!
Let your heart sing forth God's praises!
Above the uproar and noise of this world
Choosing to start your day with adoration to God
Ahead of the schedules and agendas
Singing forth in carefree melodious abandon
Arise!
To the glories of our Lord!
Break into praise and worship with joy in your heart!

A new day has dawned!
Let your praise and thanksgiving begin!
To declare the One who has saved you
The Sovereign Lord who reigns on high
Who holds all things in the hollow of His hands
Shout and declare
His majesty! His greatness!
His Love for you and me!
Our Abba Father!
The One who cares for us!
He will never leave us nor forsake us.
Should we not be grateful with a heart of thanksgiving?
Singing praises
Worshiping Him above all else?
How great thou art, O Lord!
Let our praises never cease.
May our hearts rise to thee!
In unfettered worship!

Scriptures:

- Psalm 95:6-7 – Come, let us bow down in worship, let us kneel before the Lord our Maker;…

- Psalm 96 All – For great is the Lord and most worthy of praise;…

- Psalm 98 All – Sing to the Lord a new song…shout for joy before the Lord, the King.

- Psalm 100 All – Shout for joy to the Lord, all the earth.

With praises for my King!

The Life of the Tree

The small pomegranate seedling comes to life
Foliage sparse at spring's awakening
Green appearing overnight with tiny glossy chartreuse leaves
Shining brilliantly in the warm sunshine
Clothing the tree in glorious splendor
Ruby red blossoms in stark contrast to the greenery
A tree bedecked in beauty
Yet amongst the branches spiky thorns cling amid the foliage
In time the rosy blossoms swell into tiny orbs
Month by month, they grow
Changing form, enlarging, bending branches to the ground
Ruby red fruit, a pomegranate delight!
Each piece of fruit packed with tiny succulent morsels
Juicy and sweet
Fall's harvest! God's bountiful blessing!
A reason to praise God, the Creator of all things
With a thankful heart for the life of the tree!

Then came… "a terrible wind"…
The poor tree bending low in the gale
Buffeted by gusts and blasts
Leaning sideways, touching the ground
Sapping the life from the tree
Crisp withered leaves appearing within the branches
Oh, wondrous tree! Where has your glory gone?
Are you lost? Looking so forlorn!
Can you be saved? Brought back to life?

With care the toppled tree is brought upright once again!
Lovingly secured, fed and watered
Are there signs of life within the branches?

Is there hope of a transformation?
The tap root seems intact, holding fast
Spring's awakening will tell the final truth
If the tree survives and grows once more
To produce fruit in the life of the tree!

Do not our lives take a similar path?
Toppled by worldly winds, things that don't last?
Buffeted by daily tasks and pressing chores
Needing special care and love
Needing to be saved and transformed
Changed to live a life that is vibrant and alive
Who can do such a thing in our lives?
Jesus! The One who reigns in heavenly realms!
Able to bring new life, giving hope and love
For His care transcends all our troubles and woes
He is able to aright our toppled circumstances
Those situations that seem insurmountable
Repairing our lives and bringing joy and peace once more
For Christ is so like the pomegranate tree!
Beautiful! Shining brightly in Light!
Yet wearing a crown of thorns for us
Shedding His ruby red blood for our sins
Toppled by angry men
Yet rising to resurrection life!
Providing salvation to all who believe!
Bringing fruit into the life of the believer!
Life where there was none
Oh, that we would lean on Him, our Rock and foundation!
The tap root of our spiritual life
Let us praise Him for the life He gives!

Scriptures:

- **Psalm 1:1-3** – He is like a tree planted by streams of water, which yields its fruit in season and whose leaf does not wither. Whatever he does prospers.
- **Matthew 13:3-9, 18-23** - …but since he has no root, he lasts only a short time. …But the one who received the seed… hears…understands…produces a crop.
- **John 15:1-8** - …This is to my Father's glory, that you bear much fruit, showing yourselves to be my disciples.
- **I Corinthians 3 All** - …So neither he who plants nor he who waters is anything, but only God, who makes things grow. …and you are of Christ, and Christ is of God.
- **Ephesians 3:14-21** - …I pray that you, being rooted and established in love, may have power…to grasp how wide and long and high and deep is the love of Christ,…

So grateful that I am rooted and grounded in Christ!

Mountaintop Calm

What peaceful relaxing calm can be found
Beside a scenic mountaintop lake
The glisten and sparkle of pristine cool waters
A gentle breeze ripples the shiny surface
Gentle waves lapping in rhythm onto the sandy beach
Pebbles glistening in the brilliant sunshine
A gust of wind fills the air with a rush through the pines
Sending soothing whispers across the lake
Lifting and skipping leaves along the ground
God's outdoor freshness touches your face
A fish breaches the water-top looking for bugs
While a yellow butterfly flutters in the gentle breeze
Dragonflies skim across the green-blue lake
Dipping down to touch the water below
A duck glides by and black birds flit across the sky
The air is delightfully warm
But snow still lies in crevices on distant mountain peaks
A peaceful hush…sounds echo from afar
Quietness abounds!

Where does true peace reside?
A peace and calm above the storm?
God's perfect peace which passes all understanding?
A peace, like a Holy Spirit wind, touching a silent waiting heart
Lifting and filling a hurting and sorrowing soul
Where is that calm when the churning waters rage?
Like the lake trout searching for the elusive bug…a tasty morsel.

God's perfect peace and calm can be found
Beside a mountaintop lake
But also amid the Father's Holy Word

Food for the soul, peace to the heart
As a canoe glides gracefully upon the still water
The oars digging deep, moving ever forward
God's Word directs and guides our way and our life
As we delve into His truth, seeking Christ
Our Prince of peace!
Finding peace and calm within the pages of God's Word
May we not merely skim the surface but dive deep within
Seek to find God
Desiring His very presence
Where peace and life reside
Where mountaintop calm abides
Where He is!

Scriptures:

- Psalm 19:1-4 - The heavens declare the glory of God; the skies proclaim the work of his hands.

- Psalm 23 – The LORD is my shepherd,…He makes me lie down in green pastures, he leads me beside quiet waters, he restores my soul,…

- Psalm 119:105 – Your word is a lamp to my feet and a light for my path.

- Isaiah 26:3-4 – You will keep in perfect peace him whose mind is steadfast, because he trusts in you. Trust in the LORD forever, for the LORD, the LORD, is the Rock eternal.

- Isaiah 55:6 – Seek the LORD while he may be found; call on him while he is near.

- Matthew 8:23-27 - …Then he got up and rebuked the winds and the waves, and it was completely calm.

After a peaceful mountaintop day

Nature's Praise

The heavens declare the glory of the Lord!
But a garden…
Sings forth His praises!
At the break of dawn!
Proclaiming a new day!
The birds with their melodious chirping
With cheerful praise in song
Their trill awakens the early morning rays at sunrise
Hummingbirds flitting from bush to bush
Jabbering back and forth
Playing chase across the lawn
Speaking joy and laughter
The gentle breeze in dewy coolness
Whispers through the garden paths
Around blooming bushes
With soft gentle sounds
The gladiolas stand abloom in erect rows
Like a chorus line
In beauty, they raise their blossoms heavenward
Trumpeting forth God's majesty
All day long!
Ruby amaryllis, roses and sweet smelling petunias
Shout forth praise in glory and splendor!
Feathery reeds and grasses
Swaying in graceful harmony
Dancing in tune to the wind
Bowing to the glory of God!
Uttering forth praise!
Even lizards on the garden wall
Pumping up and down in calisthenics
Proclaim God's praises
In playful chase
Expressing joy!

Life!
Does not a garden speak forth?
Peace and quiet
God's gentle whisper
His very presence
Can you not imagine?
God's Creation, the garden of Eden!
What bliss! What joy and peace!
Singing forth in wondrous praise!
Shouting forth to its Creator
God is worthy! God is worthy!
Worthy of glory, and honor and praise!
For He is above all and over all
High and lifted up in splendor and majesty!
King of kings and Lord of lords
One day we all will stand before His throne
In awe, giving forth praise to the Lord above
If a garden sings forth praise to God Most High,
Should we not do likewise?
Shouldn't we declare the worth of our Savior and Lord?
In joyful praise and song!

SCRIPTURES:

- PSALM 100 ALL — Shout for joy to the LORD, all the earth. Worship the LORD with gladness; come before him with joyful songs…for the LORD is good and his love endures forever.

- PSALM 104 ALL — …He set the earth on its foundation; it can never be moved. …How many are your works, O LORD! In wisdom you made them all; the earth is full of your creatures. …Praise the LORD, O my soul. Praise the LORD.

- PSALM 150 ALL — Praise the LORD…Let everything that has breath praise the Lord. Praise the LORD.

Thank you Lord for my garden, your wondrous creation!

Life's Simple Pleasures

God's blessings from above
Life's simple pleasures!
A gorgeous early morning sunrise
Painted with subtle colors of pinks and gold
The sound of birds filling the morning air
Singing their joyous melodious song
A hawk soaring on heavenly heights above
Catching the wind in its feathers
The sound of gentle rain hitting still water
Sending circles across the smooth surface
Thunder and lightning filling a dark stormy sky
Giving forth a spectacular display of light
Seasons in varied array
From lush green of spring to golden splendor of fall
A small child's first steps
Teetering and unsure
A little boy playing in splashing water from the hose
Trying to get his father wet
Giggling with glee
A sixteen year old teenager
Maturing with possibilities into adulthood
A birthday celebration with cake and candles aglow
The exchange of "happy birthday" wishes
Family get-togethers
Laughing and enjoying a meal around a full table
A oneness of love and family
A friend knocking at your front door unexpectedly
The joy of sharing and talking together
Friendship and togetherness
Love's embrace
Being in church surrounded by caring loving friends
Worshipping the Lord
With heavenly music and prayer

God's blessings from above
Eternal pleasures forever
Christ's sacrificial love
Extended to a sinful and an unworthy world
The blessing of God's wondrous grace
Freely given
Eternal life with the Father
The indwelling gift of His Holy Spirit
Residing within us
Giving joy
Comfort and a sense of belonging
God's Holy Word
Nurturing the heart and soul
A path and guide for living each day
God's promises
Forever true and dependable
Our sure and certain Hope
In the One who reigns forever on high!
Praise His Holy Name!
May we give thanks from a grateful heart
For God's simple pleasures and heavenly blessings from His hand!

SCRIPTURES:

- PSALM 19 ALL – The heavens declare the glory of God; the skies proclaim the work of his hands.

- PSALM 100 ALL – …For the LORD is good and his love endures forever; his faithfulness continues through all generations.

- EPHESIANS 1:3-14 – Praise be to God and the Father of our Lord Jesus Christ, who has blessed us in the heavenly realms with every spiritual blessing in Christ.

Basking in life's simple pleasures given by the Father above!

Chapter 6
God's Presence

DEUTERONOMY 31:8 – "The LORD himself goes before you and will be with you; he will never leave you nor forsake you. Do not be afraid; do not be discouraged."

PSALM 139:7-10 – Where can I go from your Spirit?
Where can I flee from your presence? If I go up to the heavens, you are there; if I make my bed in the depths, you are there. If I rise on the wings of the dawn, if I settle on the far side of the sea, even there your hand will guide me, your right hand will hold me fast.

Preface

God's presence! It is all around you. God resides in the wind, in His creation and as close as a heartbeat. But how do you know that God is present…with you? Can you feel Him or touch Him? Can we know for sure that He reside with us in the realm we live in? We can know, because God's Word proclaims His presence with believers who have put their trust and faith in God's Son, Jesus Christ. God has sent His children, another Counselor, God's Holy Spirit to reside and be with us always…His very presence to dwell within us. How cool is that! I have God's Spirit within me and He will never leave me nor forsake me.

But there are times! Don't you sometimes "feel" totally alone, lost in your heartaches and cares? Don't you sometimes ask, "Where is God when I need Him the most?"

I've been there! I think everyone has those feelings of aloneness and despair. I remember one night after I lost my husband when I cried out to the Lord in my loneliness and heartache. As I slept in the middle of the night, I was awakened by a "word". I had never used this word, didn't know what it meant and after trying unsuccessfully to go back to sleep, I finally got up and wrote the word down on a tablet. The word was "ubiquity". Wasn't sure of its spelling but thought…in the morning I will look it up and I did. The word meant…presence everywhere or in many places simultaneously…Omnipresence!

I had forgotten that God truly was with me! I was astonished to know that even in my heartache and loneliness, God had not left me alone…He was ever present with me and He allowed His Holy Spirit to burst in on my sleep to tell me that I was not alone.

Perhaps you are going through difficulties and hard things in your life, be assured…God is with you! He will make His presence known to you if you truly seek to know Him and find Him. When all seems lost…God dwells within you to comfort and enable you. Do not despair! God told Joshua, "Be strong and courageous. Do not be discouraged, for the LORD your God will be with you wherever you go." (Joshua 1) The same remains true today. God is ever present with us!

Encircled

Wrapped securely in a cozy cocoon
Encircled round about by clouds
Darkness growing in all directions
Yet held in brilliant sunshine
The blackness of the clouds
Making the sunshine even more radiant
Encapsulated in the warmth of the sun's rays
While all around the storm grows
Rain clouds
A storm on the horizon
But feeling held in the grip of God Himself
Seeing the radiance and glory of His creation
Experiencing His love and care, up close and personal
Protected from the outside world
Wrapped in a calming peace
Enjoying the awe of God's abiding presence
Oh, to remain in the light
Encircled about
And yet the storm clouds grow ever closer
Advancing upon the Holy light from above
Until the sunshine is hidden from view
The circle of light vanishing out of sight
However even though the storm rages round about
The encircling light of the One who has saved you
Is forever "with" you!

In the midst of the storms of life
The sunshine may peek out of the clouds from time to time
Fading in and out of circumstances and events
But God's light
Jesus Christ, the Light of the world

Remains forever constant shining brightly out of the darkness
Encircling you! Enveloping you!
Bringing His love and peace
Providing calm in the center of the storms of life
Giving comfort when faced with heartache
Security when overwhelmed by financial disaster
Love amid broken relationships
His presence during suffering and pain
Bringing joy out of heartbreak
Peace out of chaos
Direction and guidance by His Holy Spirit
When you are uncertain of the path to take
A plan and a purpose for living
Giving life in the face of death
Eternal life
When you surrender your life to Him
When you choose to follow in His footsteps
Encircled in His love and grace
Held within His brilliant Light
Encapsulated in Christ's loving arms
Seeing His radiance and glory
Face to face
Enjoying His all-encompassing Presence
Encircled by unending Love!
Forevermore!

SCRIPTURES:

- DEUTERONOMY 31:6,8 – The LORD himself goes before you and will be with you; he will never leave you nor forsake you. Do not be afraid; do not be discouraged.

- PSALM 34 ALL – v.7 – The angel of the LORD encamps around those who fear him, and he delivers them.

- ISAIAH 40:21-31 – "To whom will you compare me? Or who

is my equal?" says the Holy One.

- JOHN 8:12 – When Jesus spoke again to the people, he said, "I am the light of the world. Whoever follows me will never walk in darkness, but will have the light of life."
- JAMES 1:17-18 – Every good and perfect gift is from above, coming down from the Father of the heavenly lights, who does not change like shifting shadows. He chose to give us birth…
- REVELATION 22:1-7 - …They will see his face…There will be no more night. They will not need the light of a lamp or the light of the sun, for the Lord God will give them light. And they will reign for ever and ever.

Encircled in His love even in the midst of storms

The Search!

Summer is upon us!
The earth is emblazoned in summer heat.
The sun's rays baking the surrounding landscape
Cooking plants and people alike; scorching the earth
Man and beast seeking to take cover
To find a place of coolness
A respite from the day's sunny temperatures
The ants are on their tireless march
Searching, seeking water and a source of nourishment
Traveling along their mysterious path
Relentlessly invading the coolness of the house
Away from the heat of the day
Even the adventurous roaming cat
Coming in from the blazing baking sun
Seeking refuge in a spot on the cool tile floor
The gnatcatcher, on the wing, also seeking a drink
Swooping down over the cool water of the swimming pool
Quenching his thirst in the morning light
Before the heat of the long hot day
All seeking refreshment, nourishment, peace and calm
Diligent in their pursuit
Their natural inclination fulfilling God's purpose
All seeking what they need
Finding it within God's wondrous creation
God's provision in a dry and thirsty land
The mighty Provider of all things!

And yet…what of mankind's search?
The deep desires and needs of his heart and soul?
What we truly need seems so elusive and unobtainable!
Just beyond our reach

We seek that which satisfies, but in most cases, never find it.
Searching in all the wrong places
Seeking happiness in things and activities
Striving for material gain, success and money
Seeking "true" love, fulfillment and meaning to one's life
Perfect joy and peace in an imperfect world
Traveling down well-worn pathways toward oblivion
With uncertainty at every turn and unsure of the future
Roaming aimlessly and merely existing in this life
Lost and lonely
However…there is a solution for what truly satisfies!
It's not a "what", but a "Who"!
The One who fulfills the deepest desires of your heart and soul!
He is the One we truly seek and need.
God Almighty! The Sovereign One!
The Provider of all things!
Our respite in a busy world, water for our thirsty soul
Shade for the scorched and troubled heart
Joy and peace amid trying circumstances
Love, "true love" to the unloved, unlovely and unlovable
Hope and salvation for the lost and lonely
A sure promise of an eternal future home with our Savior
Seek Him while He may be found!
He is the culmination of your search for deeper meaning in life.
The Light in a dark world! The hope of every wandering heart!
Christ Jesus, the all sufficient One!

Scriptures:

- I Chronicles 28:9 – …If you seek him, he will be found by you; but if you forsake him, he will reject you forever.

- Proverbs 21:21 – He who pursues righteousness and love finds life, prosperity and honor.

- Isaiah 55 All – "Come, all you who are thirsty,…Listen, listen to me, and eat what is good,…Seek the LORD while he may be found; call on him while he is near.

- MATTHEW 7:7-12 - …For everyone who asks receives; he who seeks finds; and to him who knocks, the door will be opened.
- MATTHEW 13:44-46 – The kingdom of heaven is…like a merchant looking for fine pearls. When he found one of great value, he…sold everything he had and bought it.
- PHILIPPIANS 3:12-21 - …but I press on to take hold of that for which Christ Jesus took hold of me.
- I TIMOTHY 6:17-19 – Command those…to put their hope in God, who richly provides us with everything for our enjoyment. …so that they may take hold of the life that is truly life.

Striving to pursue God more and more in my life

In the Wind

It appears out of nowhere
Gusting below canyons down to the valley
A hard blast of southerly wind
Ushering in a change in the weather
Bending trees in its wake
Sending leaves and debris airborne
Causing pine needles to take flight midair across the sky
Leaning palm trees in a sideway slant
Their bristly fronds blown in one direction
Pointing to the winds destination
Sending birds to seek cover
To hide on tree branches or clinging to electric wires
Transporting dust and pollen
Touching face and mussing hair
The blustery wind!
Blowing strong and steady, fierce at times
Causing us to seek shelter, possibly abhorring its presence
Yet sometimes, just a gentle breeze whispering in the trees
Cool and refreshing
The breath of God upon the landscape causing us to take notice
To embrace its cleansing power
Is not God's might and power, His very presence seen?
In the wind!

What kind of wind blows into your life?
The fierce and the furious or the gentle and serene?
For into our life many influences flow
Perhaps the wind of circumstances appearing out of nowhere
Situations blasting us from all directions
Bending and sending our lives into a turmoil
Causing us to lean in their wake

Directing us down an uncertain path
Sending us to an unwanted destination
Touching our lives with the pollution of this world
Causing us to run for cover
To hide until the wind of circumstance shifts or changes
But
God is faithful!
He sends His Holy Spirit to comfort and heal
In the midst of a blustery situation
His still small voice speaks to us in gentleness and calm
Refreshing our heart and soul
The breath of the Spirit hidden in God's Word
Embracing us! Teaching us!
Changing us! Cleansing us!
Oh, that the gentle breeze of God's presence
Would blow across our lives giving us wisdom
Let us not be tossed and turned by every circumstance
But steady and unchanging
Following the God who leads us down pleasant pathways
Who makes His presence known in our life
May we seek Him
Our glorious and risen Lord
Directed and guided by the wind of His presence!

Scriptures:

- I Kings 19:1-12- …then a great and powerful wind tore the mountains apart and shattered the rocks before the LORD,… and after the fire came a gentle whisper.

- Job 32:8 – But it is the spirit in a man, the breath of the Almighty, that gives him understanding.

- Psalm 16 All – You have made known to me the path of life; you will fill me with joy in your presence, with eternal

pleasures at your right hand.
- JOHN 3:3-17 – v.8 – "The wind blows wherever it pleases. You hear its sound, but you cannot tell where it comes from or where it is going. So it is with everyone born of the Spirit."
- EPHESIANS 4:14-16 - …blown here and there by every wind of teaching…instead…we will in all things grow up into him who is the Head, that is Christ.
- II TIMOTHY 3:14-17 – All Scripture is God-breathed and is useful for teaching, rebuking, correcting and training in righteousness,…
- JAMES 1:5-8 – But when he asks, he must believe and not doubt, because he who doubts is like a wave of the sea, blown and tossed by the wind.

Tossed and turned by circumstances but secure in Christ!

Out of the Fog

The fog's firm grip hugs closely to the morning ground
    With dewy droplets descending in the air all around
Dampness clings to every living plant and tree
    Obscuring the landscape of what we could visibly see.
The dense fog hides sun, moon and stars above in the sky;
    Capturing cars, houses and roads before our eyes
The foggy stillness lays in tranquil peacefulness;
    A silent breeze moves it with serene gentle quietness.
Drifting, softly spreading it's misty wet coolness;
    To touch your cheek with a gentle subtle kiss
Early day's sun arises shining forth with brilliant rays;
    Vaguely seen, hidden by fog's morning haze.
And yet, out of the fog, sun's radiant glow slowly appears;
    Parting the dreary fog and bringing sunny cheer.
Causing fog's grip to dissipate and depart
    Bringing warmth and life to the day, a brand new start
        Out of the fog!

Sometimes, are we also caught in a similar fog and haze?
    Surrounded, engulfed by life's confusing worldly ways?
Searching for direction, caught up in doubts and strife;
    Seeking to know our purpose, God's plans for our life?
Which way should we travel; how can we know?
    How can we see in earth's fog which way to go?
But, there is One who can lead you through life's distracting maze;
    Who directs and guides you in God's holy ways.
God's Holy Spirit is given to be our constant Guide;
    Breaking through vague haziness, on whom we can rely.
His light shines where life's despairs and gloom surround
    Through Him, Christ's love to us doeth richly abound.
He leads us through dark days, uncertainty along the way;

He teaches us, consoles us, brightening our hectic day.
He shines through the darkness bringing God's holy light;
   Causing us to see more clearly, giving us surpassing sight.
We are taught and led by God's precious Word to our hearts;
   Empowered and shown God's truth, never to depart.
May we choose to rely on God's Spirit as we live out every day?
   Depending on His direction as light to lead the way
      Out of the fog!

Scriptures:

- Isaiah 48:17 -... "I am the LORD your God, who teaches you what is best for you, who directs you in the way you should go."
- John 1:4-5, 9 - ...that light was the light of men. The light shines in the darkness…
- John 8:12 -… "I am the light of the world. Whoever follows me will never walk in darkness, but will have the light of life."
- John 14:23-26 - …But the Counselor, the Holy Spirit, whom the Father will send in my name, will teach you all things and will remind you of everything I have said to you.
- Acts 1:8 - But you will receive power when the Holy Spirit comes on you;…
- Romans 8:1-17 – Life through the Spirit

Seeking to see clearly in the power of the Holy Spirit

Snow's Dusting

Morning dawn breaks crisp and cold
You can see your breath in the air.
Yesterday's passing storm has quickly departed
A distant panorama of mountain peaks
Partially hidden in lingering puffy clouds
White cotton pillow softness clinging to cold stark granite cliffs
The sun arises pushing back the cloud covering
More and more majestic mountains are revealed
Cold whiteness everywhere
The storms deliverance of pristine fresh snow
Rocks dusted in soft gentleness
Pine trees turned to shimmering crystal shapes
Covered under snow's frosty blanket
Gripping rocks, falling deep into crevices
Sparkling white, pure and clean
Untouched
Snow's dusting!
Slowly the sun moves upward on the horizon
Its warm rays penetrating earth and sky
Snow's dusting dwindles in small measure
A little at a time, ever-melting before the heat of the day
Falling from trees, evaporating
Only shaded and protected patches remain
Only within the deep crevices on the highest rocky cliffs
Until God sends another snowy day
Once again darkening the sky
Bringing clouds in the wake of the storm
And once more it happens!
Snow's dusting!

Life's dusting!
God's Holy Spirit like snow from heaven
Dusting our lives with God's Holy Presence
Gently indwelling every crevice within
Guiding, directing, teaching, convicting of sin
Covering our lives with His sweet comfort
Speaking softly in His quiet whisper
Letting us know that God resides within our hearts
And yet…the world interrupts our vision
Distracting, squelching
Causing us to be caught up in daily busyness and turmoil
Melting away any evidence of God's Holy Spirit
Only in the deep recesses of our soul
Doth God's Spirit still remain
His Voice quenched
Inaudible
Until
God sends the storms of life.
How quickly we seek the comfort of His Holy Spirit?
Our need draws us to Himself.
And God is faithful!
He meets us right where we are.
Filling us once more
Forgiving our sin
Cleansing us and making us holy
Acceptable in His sight
Indwelt with His Spirit
Graced by His Presence
Once more…dusted by His love!

Scriptures:

- Isaiah 11:1-2 - …The Spirit of the LORD will rest on him (Christ)…

- JOHN 16:5-15 – "…But when he, the Spirit of truth, comes, he will guide you into all truth."
- I CORINTHIANS 2:9-16 - …but God has revealed it to us by His Spirit.
- GALATIANS 5:16-25 - …Since we live by the Spirit, let us keep in step with the Spirit.
- EPHESIANS 1:13-14 - …you are marked in him with a seal, the promised Holy Spirit,…
- EPHESIANS 4:30; I THESSALONIANS 5:19 – And do not grieve the Holy Spirit of God,…

Grateful for God's dusting of His Spirit in my life.

Quiet Splendor

Hush!
Can you hear the quietness of the day?
Or
Does the world blare loudly in your ears?
Hush!
Can you hear a snowflake
Drifting downward to touch the ground?
Softly, gently,
Without a sound
Perhaps the hush of wind in the trees rustling in the leaves
Hardly heard and barely seen
The moon rising on a starry night, giving no sound
Only radiant light
The quietness found while a baby slumbers
The stillness in the house late at night
When all the lights are out
Where lays that quiet splendor?
That still small voice
Speaking softly to our hearts?

What prevents you from finding that place of quietness?
That place of stillness deep within your soul
God's calming peace
Quiet communion with your Lord
The Creator of all things
The One who desires to spend time with you
Quiet, unbroken togetherness
In solitude and prayer
Alone in quiet splendor!

Do the demands of the day fill your attention?

Work and busyness
Computers and cell phones
Children and household chores
Recreation
Frustrations and pressures
Life in general
No time
Stealing your quiet time
Can you not find time for God?
Can you not steal away into His Presence?

For God invites
He beckons you to come
Hush, be still my soul!
For God offers
Peace and comfort
His never-ending love
His Holy Word as our guide for each day
To light our path
The Holy Spirit
His still quiet voice to our heart
His sweet communion
He is there!
Whenever we choose to show up!
"Come!"
Enter into His sanctuary
Enter into His quiet Splendor!

SCRIPTURES:

- PSALM 16:11 – You have made known to me the path of life; you will fill me with joy in your presence, with eternal pleasures at your right hand.

- PSALM 23 ALL - …he leads me beside quiet waters, he restores my soul.

- Zephaniah 3:17 – "The LORD your God is with you, he is mighty to save. He will take great delight in you, he will quiet you with his love, he will rejoice over you with singing."
- Matthew 28-30 – "Come unto me, all you who are weary and burdened, and I will give you rest…."
- I Thessalonians 4:11-12 – Make it your ambition to lead a quiet life,…

May God quiet my heart so I can hear Him.

U – B – I – Q – U – I – T – Y

Webster's Dictionary – **ubiquity** – n. everywhere; presence everywhere or in many places simultaneously; OMNIPRESENCE

There is nowhere that God is not!
He is ever present
Omnipresent
Ubiquitous
He is the farthest far
He is the nearest near.
He is beyond any star.
He is as close as a breath.
He is all around us
Do you feel His presence?

He is the WHO, WHAT, WHY, WHERE, WHEN and HOW
Of all creation
Present in everything we see and touch
In the glorious sunrise
The wondrous clouds skirting across the sky
In the vibrant red petals of a rose, delicate and fragrant
In the purple iridescent beauty of a blooming orchid tree
In the wind rustling through the treetops
In the majestic mountains covered in white winter snow
Quiet lakes and rushing rivers
The expansive ocean, crashing to the shore
God's ubiquity before our eyes
A visual view of WHO He is!
Beyond our understanding or comprehension
We are the WHAT and the WHY
The object and the purpose of His presence
For before times beginning God had us in His mind

He formed and fashioned us into being
He desires above all things to have a relationship with us;
Through faith in the person of His own Son, Jesus Christ
Who lived and died and rose again
Providing us a way into God's very presence
For God's desire is to be close to us
By the power of His Holy Spirit, He can reside within us
God's ubiquity up close and personal

And His presence is not limited by space and time
WHERE and WHEN?
In the night-watches of the night
At the bedside of a sick child or dying loved one
In the loneliness of your life
In the emptiness of losing a spouse
In the heartbreak of a home foreclosure
When you are forced to move again
When you come to the end of the month
And there is no food for your family.
Through difficulties and life's challenges in the midst of uncertainty
For the homeless, the lost and confused, the imprisoned
Wherever and whenever
His presence is there, right beside you
Surrounding you with His ubiquity
His omnipresence

HOW is God's presence possible?
How can we know He is there?
With God…all things are possible.
Because God is God and He is faithful to His children!
Loving and kind to those whom He loves
For He will never leave us nor forsake us
He is true to His Word and His presence is assured
He is able to do all things by His power and supreme might

His presence is ever with us.
For He is God Almighty
Ubiquitous! Omnipresent!
He is God of All!
Do you know Him? He is here! Reach out into His Presence.

SCRIPTURES:

- DEUTERONOMY 31:6 – "…for the Lord your God goes with you; he will never leave you nor forsake you."

- PSALM 139 ALL - O Lord, …Where can I go from your Spirit? Where can I flee from your presence? …When I awake I am still with you.

- JOHN 1:3 – Through him all things were made; without him nothing was made that has been made.

- REVELATION 22:13 – "I am the Alpha and the Omega, the First and the Last, the Beginning and the End."

Awed by God's Presence

Vanishing

Summer is coming!
Longer days, milder nights
The warmth of the sun
The mountains declare its coming
Day by day the snow is vanishing
The fluffy whiteness on the mountaintops melting
Visibly less and less from afar
Succumbing to the sun's radiant rays
Only stubborn patches of ice remain in the crevices
Solid and translucent, deeply ingrained
Hidden and clinging to the granite cliffs
Shaded in the shadows
And yet the sun's light finally reaching deep within
Exposing the rock face
All trace of snow and ice, winter's cold
Will vanish away!
Only the strong, stark mountain rocks remain
Standing tall, erect against the blue sky
Immovable, steady and unchanging
Yet marred by erosion and weather
Only winter's snowfall has vanished
Vanishing in the wake of God's presence!

And so it is in the life of a believer in the wake of God's presence
For as we come to know Christ in our life
God changes us, transforms us by His Holy Spirit
Day by day melting away the fluff in our lives
The non-consequential and the things displeasing to God
Those sins appearing less and less
As the radiance of God's Word shines into our lives
Changing our appearance, impacting our behavior

His light shines in the darkness, exposing the inner parts
And yet
There are the stubborn sins and heart attitudes remaining
Ingrained in the deep recesses of our lives
Hidden to outsiders but not from God
Clinging in the shadows in the crevices of our heart
But God's light penetrates within to sanctify us
In every part
Transforming us into a new creation
Causing us to stand in holiness and purity
Steadfast, albeit weathered and marred
The consequences of sin
But as God's presence resides more and more
Our lives are a reflection
Being molded into Christ-likeness
Able to stand tall and erect before the judgment seat of God
Holy and acceptable
For Christ, in love, has redeemed and purified us
Taken our sin upon Himself and has forgiven us
Our sin has been cleansed by his blood
Vanished forever!

Scriptures:

- Psalm 103 all – v. 12 – …as far as the east is from the west, so far has he removed our transgressions from us.

- John 1:1-5 – in him was life, and that life was the light of men. The light shines in the darkness,…

- I Corinthians 16:13-14 – be on your guard; stand firm in the faith; be men of courage; be strong. Do everything in love.

- II Corinthians 3:18 – and we, who with unveiled faces all reflect the Lord's glory, are being transformed into his likeness with ever-increasing glory, which comes from the Lord, who is the Spirit.

- II CORINTHIANS 5:16-21 - …if anyone is in Christ, he is a new creation;…God made him who had no sin to be sin for us, so that in him we might become the righteousness of God.
- EPHESIANS 5:1-21 - …For it is the light that makes everything visible…be filled with the Spirit.
- HEBREWS 4:12-13 – for the word of God …penetrates even to dividing soul and spirit…it judges the thoughts and attitudes of the heart. Nothing in all creation is hidden from God's sight.
- HEBREWS 12:1-13 - …discipline…produces a harvest of righteousness and peace for those who have been trained by it.

Being sanctified day by day

Butterfly Bliss

There they are!
In the early morning sunshine
Butterflies in abundance
Floating, fluttering and flapping their colorful wings
Drifting effortlessly through the air
Beautiful grace in vivid coloring
Orange, yellow and red
Sometimes exotic colors of blue, purple and green
Some small and ornately insignificant
Others uniquely designed like the swallowtail
Skirting about the garden
All seeking precious nectar
Drawn to the flowery shrubs and sweet smelling flowers
Alighting here and there
Coming back time and time again
Drinking in the sweet ambrosia
Fluttering onward to the next blossom
Flitting helter-skelter on the gentle breeze
Intertwined in harmony with God's creation
Blissfully going on their way
Enjoying the day from flower to flower!

Oh, that we also would bask in that glorious bliss!
Where all is provided
Where the cares of the world are left behind
Drifting effortlessly through life
Floating blissfully on our busy way
In perfect harmony with God and man
Enjoying the day!

In full assurance
In contrast to the circumstances surrounding us
The world and all the strains of life
Seeking and desiring a place of deepest joy!
A place of serenity and peace
Quietness
Having unity and oneness with God
Delighting in His very presence
Finding rest for our souls
Comfort and strength
Available to all that would seek Him
Where the Lord gives to all who truly hunger and thirst
Showing no favoritism
A place where we can take in
The sweet nectar of His glorious Word
A place of refreshment
Far from the stress of this world
Gently drawn away by God's Holy Spirit
To the feet of Jesus
There to repose and stay awhile
To learn of Him
To commune and talk with Him
Time and time again
To reside in His blissfulness
To see Him face to face
Oh, glorious day!
To bask in the wonder of His Presence!

SCRIPTURES:

- PSALM 19 ALL – v. 7- The law of the LORD is perfect, reviving the soul.

- ISAIAH 40:28-31 – v.31- …But those who hope in the LORD will renew their strength,…

- MATTHEW 11:28-30 – "Come to me…and you will find rest for your souls."
- LUKE 10:39-42 - …Mary who sat at the Lord's feet listening to what he said. "…Mary has chosen what is better, and it will not be taken away from her."
- JOHN 6:44-51 – "No one can come to me unless the Father who sent me draws him,…"
- I PETER 10L19-25 - …let us draw near to God with a sincere heart in full assurance of faith,…

Finding rest at the feet of Jesus

-Distractions-

Can you see Him?
Can you feel His presence surrounding you?
Almighty God! The great "I am"!
The Author and Creator of all life
Seen in a myriad of ways in the world around us
Making His awesome presence known to us
In the glory of a sunrise through shafts of sunlight
Beams drifting downward amid dark storm clouds
In the majesty of towering mountains firmly planted
In stately redwood trees rising ever skyward
In the flutter of a delicate hummingbird's wings
Seen in the splendor of a dazzling red rose
Bedecked with sparkling dewdrops on its velvety petals
Visible in the gentleness of a sleeping child
Softly cradled in quiet slumber
Recognizable in circumstances
When impossible situations are changed
In answer to fervent prayers
Seen in His provisions and loving care
Ever present in the lives of His children who belong to Him
Available and approachable
Our "Abba" Father!

What hinders us from communion with our Loving Lord?
What deters us from time alone with Him?
What leads us far from His presence?
Distractions!
In a world fraught with…schedules, agendas and chores
Demands of our time and effort
Technology, Ipods, cell phones and the like
Leading us to the present, urging us away from the eternal

Sports, entertainment, fun and enjoyment, taking up our time
Momentary events that lead us nowhere
Does all this seem harsh and biased?
In and of themselves, these distractions are part of our everyday.
God has placed us in this world to live life
But…not to the exclusion of Himself!
All this is worldly drawing us away from God on a regular basis
Distracting us from the One who is Holy!
Even our religiosity distracts
Rituals, customs, institutions, debates over music styles
The way we've always done it!
Caught in the hum-drum going through the motions
Hindered and distracted away by wandering thoughts
Drawn away from true worship
From seeing and embracing, The Living Lord!
For what are distractions in the Christian life?
A drawing away from…The One who is worthy!
Distracted away from Jesus!
Do you want to see the Father then look to God's beloved Son!
Focus your eyes on Jesus, the Author and Perfecter of your faith
Don't cast your eyes aside, look on Him!
Embrace Christ, your Savior and Redeemer!
For He is humble and lowly in heart
Cast your gaze on Him
Let Him be your distraction from the world around.
Come into His glorious presence, seeing Him, face to face!
Don't be distracted away!

Scriptures:

- Hosea 6:1-3 – "Come, let us return to the LORD…that we may live in his presence."

- Matthew 11:25-30 – "Come to me…for I am gentle and humble in heart and you will find rest for your souls.

- JOHN 14:6-7 – Jesus answered, "I am the way and the truth and the life. No one comes to the Father except through me."
- TITUS 2:11-15 – For the grace of God that brings salvation has appeared to all men. It teaches us to say "No" to ungodliness and worldly passions…while we wait for the blessed hope—the glorious appearing of our great God and Savior, Jesus Christ
- HEBREWS 1:3 – The Son is the radiance of God's glory and the exact representation of his being, sustaining all things by his powerful word.
- HEBREWS 12:2-3 – Let us fix our eyes on Jesus, the author and perfecter of our faith,…consider him…
- JAMES 1:26-27 - …Religion that God our Father accepts as pure and faultless is this:…to keep oneself from being polluted by the world.

Daily desiring to fix my eyes on Christ

"Above the Clouds"

The sky is full with clouds descending
Stormy black and threatening
Swollen with moisture, rain soon to come
Yet
Rays of glorious sunshine shining through patches of blue
Streaming downward in varied directions
Beams of sunlight touching the earth
Making a patchwork quilt upon the landscape
Sunshine and shadow, light and darkness
Vibrant clarity versus muted colors, shades of gray
But soar above the clouds and shadows
The light is ever brilliant and aglow
The sun's rays reach unheeded
Stretching outward to the horizon and the heavens above
Shining in glory
No clouds forbidding the sun's radiance
The shadows and the darkness lay stretched out below
Like a dense carpet
The light of the glorious sun
Reflective and bouncing upward to the sky above
All rests in calm and quietness above the clouds!
And so, God's grace shines on us all!
Amidst the shadows of everyday living, His light ever shines
Upon whatever looks dark and stormy
The hardships and challenges of life
The heartache and pain
Schedules and things to be done
In the face of worries and concerns
Distractions, demands and difficulties
Even when loss and death come into our life
God is there!

Ever present in time of trouble
He is comforting, consoling and able to understand
The rays of His presence touch us in faithful love
"Immanuel", God with us!
His light shining out of the darkness and gloom
Bringing clarity and purpose to our lives
Gracing us with His love and care
In the face of circumstances
Touching our lives with His powerful Holy Spirit
Causing us to walk in the sunlight of His Word
Helping us to stand firm
Even when we feel overwhelmed, we are led into His Light
As we seek and draw near to Him
He leads us along pathways of His choosing
Causing us to follow Him
Dependent upon the Lord for every step we take
For His way is perfect leading to eternal life in Him!
Into His presence! Into the Light of His glory!
There to reside forevermore!
Above the clouds!

Scriptures:

- **Deuteronomy 33:26-27** - "There is no one like the God of Jeshurun, who rides on the heavens to help you and on the clouds in his majesty. The eternal God is your refuge, and underneath are the everlasting arms.

- **Psalm 46 All** – God is our refuge and strength, an ever-present help in trouble. ….."Be still, and know that I am God;…" The Lord Almighty is with us;…

- **Psalm 108:1-6** - …For great is your love, higher than the heavens; your faithfulness reaches to the skies.

- **Isaiah 42:16** - …I will turn the darkness into light before them

and make the rough places smooth.
- MATTHEW 1:22-23 - …"The virgin will be with child and will give birth to a son, and they will call him Immanuel"—which means, "God with us."
- JOHN 1:1-5 – In the beginning was the Word,…In him was life, and that life was the light of men.
- II CORINTHIANS 1:3-11 – Praise be to the God and Father of our Lord Jesus Christ, …who comforts us in all our troubles,…
- II THESSALONIANS 2:13-17 – Stand firm! …loved by the Lord… God chose you to be saved…He called you…So then…stand firm and hold to the teachings we passed on to you…May our Lord Jesus Christ…who loved us…encourage your hearts and strengthen you…

The encouragement that I need when I am overwhelmed!

Dance of the Butterfly

What a delight!
Watching its delicate wings flit across the yard
In the cool hours of the quiet morning
In grace and beauty
A vibrant yellow and black swallowtail butterfly
Skipping, gliding, bouncing up and down
Graceful like a feather in the gentle breeze
Stopping to gather pollen
Here and there amongst the blossoms
Alighting upon the cement
To drink in water left in the cracks of the concrete
Drinking in deeply the moisture
Lingering, staying awhile
Enjoying the peacefully serene garden
Meandering unfettered through the flowers
Dancing back and forth
A wondrous sight!
Part of God's glorious creation
Visible and available to be seen and enjoyed
To draw our eyes to God, the Creator
To give praise and glory to Him!
Can you only imagine our future hope and joy?
Awaiting those who love the Lord!
Around the throne of grace
Before Christ, the Savior of all mankind
Jesus, clothed in majesty and might
Grace-filled and beautiful!
We will drink in the glory of the moment
Basking in the Light of His countenance
Lingering, staying awhile for all of eternity!
Enjoying His presence forever!

Unfettered, free and unencumbered by sin and despair
With not a tear in our eyes
Surrounded by God's peace and serenity
Forgiven and truly alive
Dancing before the King of kings and Lord of lords!
What joy awaits us!
To behold the wondrous sight of heaven
Visible and available to be seen and enjoyed
Drawing our eyes to God, the Creator in awe and reverence
To give praise and glory to Him!
Like the dance of the butterfly
We will joyfully dance in jubilation forevermore!
Will you be there? Do you know Jesus as your Savior?
Have you come to the Cross of Christ?
With a repentant heart, receiving His salvation
If not, why not?
For Christ's desire is a relationship with you!
To know you! Come! While there is still time!
What joy awaits you in the presence of the Lord!
Hallelujah! For our Lord God Almighty reigns.
Rejoice and be glad and give Him glory!

SCRIPTURES:

- PSALM 30:11-12 – You turned my wailing into dancing;…that my heart may sing to you and not be silent. O LORD my God, I will give you thanks forever.

- PSALM 149:1-5 - …Let them praise his name with dancing and make music to him with tambourine and harp.

- ISAIAH 6:1-8 - …I saw the LORD seated on a throne, high and exalted… "Holy, holy, holy is the LORD Almighty; the whole earth is full of his glory."

- JOHN 10: 25-30 – Jesus answered, … "My sheep listen to my

voice; I know them, and they follow me. I give them eternal life, and they shall never perish; no one can snatch them out of my hand."

- II PETER 3:8-13 - …The Lord…is patient with you, not wanting anyone to perish, but everyone to come to repentance.
- REVELATION 19-22 ALL - … "Hallelujah! For our Lord God Almighty reigns. … "It is done. I am the Alpha and the Omega, the Beginning and the End. To him who is thirsty I will give to drink without cost from the spring of the water of life.

Waiting for the Lord's return to be in His presence!

Foggy Days

The day began sunny
Sparkling bright and clear
Birds chirping in the trees with glee
Until the gray fog appeared.
Moving, drifting, taking the sun away
Hiding the sunshine, the warmth of the day
Creeping slowly atop the damp ground
Until only shadows and gloom surround.
Causing the light to recede and fade.
Clouding the day and all that God made

What is clouding your vision, obscuring your view?
Preventing you from seeing each day, fresh and new?
Blocking the possibilities of a brand new day?
Stopping you from seeing God and following His way
Perhaps your life is clouded with heartache and despair.
Financial worries or challenging health cares
Maybe you're engulfed with loneliness and depression.
Or family conflict without any resolution
Whatever has clouded your path and your way
God has the answer… to each foggy day!

For even when your way is dark and cold
Jesus' love rests within the foggy fold.
In the midst of your pain and despair;
You still remain within His loving care.
For He can lead you to quiet waters still;
Or guide you up a daunting hill.
He can calm your every waking care;
And in His presence you can share.
For His Word encourages both heart and soul;

Bringing peace and joy and hope untold
He is close to you…oh, so near;
He can cast away your every fear.
When you cling to Him in your foggy days;
He can change the gloom to His sunny Way.
For where the Lord is, there is no dark, only light.
He is right beside you…within your sight.
The fog will lift, the sun will shine;
For God is faithful…all the time!

Step into His glorious Light!
Out of the fog!

Scriptures:

- Psalm 34:18 – The LORD is close to the brokenhearted and saves those who are crushed in spirit.

- Psalm 40:1-5 – Blessed is the man who makes the LORD his trust.

- Psalm 63:1-8 - …My soul clings to you; your right hand upholds me.

- Isaiah 61:1-3 - …to bestow on them…a garment of praise instead of a spirit of despair.

- I Peter 2:9 – But you are a chosen people,…who called you out of darkness into his wonderful light.

- I Peter 5:7 – Cast all your anxiety on him because he cares for you.

Clinging to God on foggy days!

Chapter 7
God's Power

I Chronicles 29:11-13 – Yours, O LORD, is the greatness and the power and the glory and the majesty and the splendor, for everything in heaven and earth is yours. Yours, O LORD, is the kingdom; you are exalted as head over all. Wealth and honor come from you; you are the ruler of all things. In your hands are strength and power to exalt and give strength to all. Now, our God, we give you thanks, and praise your glorious name.

Preface

There is no one more powerful than God! He is King of kings and LORD of lords and He reigns forever and forever! No one can thwart His reign nor diminish His power to rule on high! Whether you believe this or not, it is altogether true. I know that many people think that they are masters of their own destiny but if God is in control and rules over all, this is a complete fallacy. God is completely sovereign and in control and HE IS THE KING OVER ALL THE UNIVERSE!

How do we see His great power in its workings in the world today? Consider the universe, the stars and planets, the galaxies reaching out into space from the earth. What power keeps everything in alignment and who makes the sun to shine and the seasons come and go? God does! God overrules His creation and keeps all things orderly within His realm.

Even in days past, God's power was evident when He caused the great flood in Noah's day (Genesis 6-8) and also when He parted the Red Sea during the Israelite's exodus from Egypt (Exodus 14). Who is able to do such things except the all powerful One, God Almighty? And in Jesus' time, great miracles were accomplished through the power of God. God still has that power to do miracles in our world today. He is able to heal the sick, change seemingly impossible circumstances and answer the most humble prayer. His power is without limit! With God, all things are possible!

Unfortunately, we are the ones that limit God by not believing that He is able to do all things; for He truly is able to do immeasurably more than all we ask or imagine, according to his power that is at work within us (Ephesians 3:20). We, as His children, have access to the power of God through the indwelling Holy Spirit. God is able to strengthen us when we feel weak, He is able to empower us to do great things for His kingdom and He is able to cause us to be bold as a witness for Christ to those whom we meet. What a resource we have to change the world! We can latch onto the power of God which is limitless. God is the Almighty One, the Sovereign Lord who reigns forever with power and strength!

A Mighty Wind

You can hear it rustling through the treetops
Filling the air with its windy roar
Blowing, whooshing through the branches
Coming down the canyons touching everything in its wake
Bending trees to their limit
Breaking off dead limbs and small branches
Sending leaves in all directions
Mighty!
Unstoppable and forceful
Making it hard to stand against the gale
Mussing one's hair
Tossing debris airborne, making a mess of the garden
Yet purifying the air and dispelling the haze
Bringing a freshness to our day
Invigorating our spirit
God's mighty wind!

Do you hear Him?
All around you; He is ever present.
In your life and all creation
Surrounding you right where you are!
On the mountain high and even in the valleys low of life
Touching everything with His power and might
Bending and breaking strongholds that engulf you
Areas of sin and rejection within your rebellious ways
Helping you to overcome and live victorious, day by day
Dispelling unrighteousness from your life
His mighty force is greater than Satan's grip
Unstoppable! All powerful!
Fortifying you to stand firm in your faith
Tossing the worthless debris out of your life

Purifying you
Bringing newness of life
Righteousness and clarity
Enlivening you spiritually by the power of His Word
Giving direction and guidance by His Holy Spirit
How great is our God!
Mighty in power and majesty! Ruler over all things!
King of kings and Lord of lords!
Would we not kneel before Him to give Him honor and praise?
Would we not cling to Him for strength and empowerment?
Where else can we go?
For He holds the keys to life eternal
He is our Rock and Redeemer. He is like a Mighty Wind.
Come! Embrace Him for who He is.
The Mighty One!

Scriptures:

- **Deuteronomy 10:12-22** - …For the LORD your God is God of gods and Lord of lords, the great God, mighty and awesome,…He is your praise; he is your God,…

- **Psalm 50:1-6** – The Mighty One, God, the LORD, speaks and summons the earth from the rising of the sun to the place where it sets.

- **Psalm 147:5** – Great is our Lord and mighty in power; his understanding has no limit.

- **Isaiah 9:6-7** - …And he will be called Wonderful Counselor, Mighty God, Everlasting Father, Prince of Peace,

- **Jeremiah 32:17-27** - "Ah, Sovereign LORD, you have made the heavens and the earth by your great power and outstretched arm. Nothing is too hard for you." …Then the word of the LORD came to Jeremiah: "I am the LORD, the God of all mankind. Is anything too hard for me?"

- EPHESIANS 1:18-23 – ...that you may know...his incomparably great power for us who believe. That power is like the working of his mighty strength, which he exerted in Christ when he raised him from the dead and seated him at his right hand in the heavenly realms,...
- EPHESIANS 3:20 – Now to him who is able to do immeasurably more than all we ask or imagine, according to his power...
- HEBREWS 7:25 – Therefore he (Christ) is able to save completely those who come to God through him, because he always lives to intercede for them.

How mighty is our God on high!

Beyond Greatness

They stand majestic and stately.
Reaching toward the sky, strong and erect
Aged in time
Sequoia gigantean
Big Trees, the giant Sequoia
Massive, standing firm and growing tall
Year upon year
Shading woodsy ground and damp earth below
Home to moss and lichen
Trees in clusters growing from root burls
Sheltering all manner of wildlife;
Graceful deer with fawns roaming free
Brilliant colored yellow banana slugs
Skunks and darting chipmunks and squirrels
Squawking blue jays
Powerful and gliding eagles alight on the treetops
Quiet stillness, in hushed silence
In grandeur they stand
Beyond greatness!

What can compare?
God can!
Awesome in majesty!
Secure and unfailing in all His ways
Immortal, eternal, beyond time and space
Strong and stately
Our Rock and Redeemer
Shelter from life's storms
Home for our heart
With mighty power
Able to bring freedom and life to all who believe

Quiet and peace to our soul
Security

Let us stand firm!
In the strength of the One who is able to do all things
Who stands immovable!
Let us stand!
Living and breathing according to God's righteous Word
Let us stand!
Upon the only One, Christ, our risen Savior
Who stands in our stead!
Giving mercy and grace
Who is beyond Greatness!

SCRIPTURES:

- PSALM 1 ALL – Blessed is the man…his delight is in the law of the Lord…He is like a tree planted by streams of water… plus Jeremiah 17:8

- PSALM 40:2 - …he set my feet on a rock and gave me a firm place to stand.

- ISAIAH 7:9B – If you do not stand firm in your faith, you will not stand at all.

- ISAIAH 40:8 - …the word of our God stands forever.

- I CORINTHIANS 16:13, GALATIANS 5:1, EPHESIANS 6:10-18 AND II THESSALONIANS 2:15 – Stand firm

- II TIMOTHY 2:19 – Nevertheless, God's solid foundation stands firm, sealed with this inscription: "The Lord knows those who are his," and "Everyone who confesses the name of the Lord must turn away from wickedness."

Standing firm upon His power and greatness!

-Mockingbird Taunt-

I hear them, even before the sun crests over the horizon!
Their varied melody wafting along on the breeze
Waking everyone to a brand new day
The mockingbirds are building a nest.
They are vigilant…busy.
Taking twigs and moss from a nearby hanging basket.
Back and forth, bringing their makings to the nest
They are extremely protective, obscurely hiding their nest
Deep within a side-yard bush, high up and unreachable
Meanwhile…the cat leisurely watches inside the house
Sitting by the back glass patio door
Taking in their comings and goings
The birds are bold…brazen…taunting!
Coming up the sidewalk hopping directly in front of the door
Knowing somehow that the cat is behind the glass
Spreading their wings wide
Fluffing their feathers in flaunting gestures
Chirping in mocking defiance
As if to say to the cat…"We dare you"
"Come on cat, come out and see what will happen."
"Don't just sit there watching."
"If you come out…we will have an opportunity to peck you."
"Bombard your head" "Swoop and dive at your tail"
"To aggravate you" "We are waiting for our moment"
Meanwhile…the cat only watches
Seemingly ignoring the bird's taunts
Safe within the confines of the serene house
Not listening nor taking notice
Secure within his haven and finally falling asleep at peace!
While the birds keep flying around in disarray!
Still there, still taunting!

Is that not what the world does?
Right before our eyes, waiting to entice
Satan's schemes to draw us out
Mocking us with brazen, bold and sinful seduction
Appealing and attractive schemes coming from every direction
Bombarding us in the news media or by way of television
Touching our lives in books, over the internet and politics
Subtle aggression waiting for us to compromise
Attacking our values and drawing us into complacency
Ready to pounce on us at every opportunity
How can we overcome the taunts of this world?
How can we be strong against the temptations of life?
Standing firm for what is right and just?

By remaining secure in the Father's care
By not listening to Satan's enticing lies
By ignoring the seductive pleasures of this life
But rather cling to the One who gives eternal life
For as we read and apply God's Word
We are able to see the world's deception
For God's Word is truth giving light and wisdom
Discernment and understanding
When faced by the world's temptations
We are able to stand firm with righteous conviction
And God's loving arms surround us
We can rest secure within His embrace.
We can find rest for our weary souls.
A safe haven!
For in this world you will have trouble
But take heart! Christ has overcome the world!

Scriptures:

- Psalm 46:1-3 – God is our refuge and strength, an ever-present

help in trouble.
- JOHN 16:33 - ...take heart! I have overcome the world."
- II CORINTHIANS 10:2-6 – For though we live in the world, we do not wage war as the world does. ...we take captive every thought to make it obedient to Christ.
- I PETER 5:8-9 - Be self-controlled and alert. Your enemy the devil prowls around like a roaring lion looking for someone to devour. Resist him, standing firm...
- I JOHN 2:15-17 - ...If anyone loves the world, the love of the Father is not in him.
- I JOHN 3:1 – How great is the love the Father has lavished on us, that we should be called children of God!
- I JOHN 4:4 - ...the one who is in you is greater than the one who is in the world.

Trusting God to keep me secure

Above the Fray

Unbelievably beautiful!
An amazing red-tailed hawk!
So unexpected, for their domain is usually on heights above
But today, down on the valley floor
In the middle of the street hopping freely along the pavement
Drinking water out of a puddle
With vibrant wings of reddish and brown hues
Feathers aglow in the sunlight
With grace and beauty, majestic and regal
Showing strength and determination
Unafraid
Causing one to stop in amazement and awe
Yet seemingly out of place
Then suddenly taking flight in one fell swoop
Expansive wings outstretched
Gaining height with a surge of his powerful wings
Soaring upward into the azure sky above
Quickly disappearing out of sight
Above the fray!

Oh, that we could soar on eagle's wings!
Oh…but, we can!
This life for today is but for a moment
We were made to reside in the heavenly realms
"With Christ"
Above the fray!

But, you say…I'm not there yet!
Today, I'm dealing with all kinds of things in my life.
Heartbreak and loneliness, pain and suffering
Financial woes and bankruptcy

Despair and hopelessness, anxiety over world affairs
Car problems, children problems, personal problems
And the list goes on…
I'm down in the valley, not in the heavenly realms
However…there is hope for today!
Even in the valley of life itself, our hope rests in Christ alone
On Him we can lean
He is our solid Rock on whom we can stand
Standing firm in the midst of circumstances
He is our strong tower
To whom we can run in the face of trials and difficulties
He is living water to our soul in whom we can be refreshed
By His Holy Word, He teaches and encourages us
His Holy Spirit guides and directs us in His ways
He is the One we look to for comfort, care and love
In whom we can find rest for our weary heart
He is faithful, trustworthy and He hears our every concern
Even when we are down in the valley of despair
He causes our hearts to mount up on the wings of eagles
To soar into the heavenly realms
To live victoriously!
Above the fray!

Scriptures:

- Psalm 17:6-9 - …keep me as the apple of your eye; hide me in the shadow of your wings…

- Psalm 18:1-6 - …The LORD is my rock, my fortress and my deliverer; my God is my rock, in whom I take refuge,…

- Psalm 91 All – He who dwells in the shelter of the Most High will rest in the shadow of the Almighty. …He will cover you with his feathers, and under his wings you will find refuge; his faithfulness will be your shield and rampart.

- PROVERBS 18:10 – The name of the LORD is a strong tower; the righteous run to it and are safe.

- ISAIAH 40:25-31 - …but those who hope in the LORD will renew their strength. They will soar on wings like eagles; they will run and not grow weary, they will walk and not be faint.

- MATTHEW 11:28-30 – "Come to me, all you who are weary and burdened, and I will give you rest."

- JOHN 4:7-14 - …Jesus answered,… "Indeed, the water I give him will become in him a spring of water welling up to eternal life."

- HEBREWS 12:1-3 - …Let us fix our eyes on Jesus, the author and perfecter of our faith…

Resting in the shelter of the Most High God!
        Soaring on the heights with Christ!

The Battle

A pleasant moment in the sun
The patio warm with a gentle cooling breeze
Then unexpectedly, out of nowhere
A healthy brown lizard racing at my feet
Scampering quickly across the patio
Making a beeline to the other side
Focused on an object within his sights
Rummaging in the flower bed
The battle is on! The struggle has begun!
A healthy green tomato worm with a pointed red horn on top
In the lizard's grasp
The lizard is determined
The tomato worm twisting, writhing
Mouth opened wide trying to escape
But held secure within the lizard's mouth
Not letting go of his prey
Racing off to eat his tempting delight
Great fare for a lizard; not so, for the tomato worm
The battle ended with the lizard, the victor!
What amazement and wonder amid God's wondrous creation
Survival of the fittest!
Engaged in the battle!

Are we not equally engaged in battle?
Out of nowhere the tempter comes!
Enticing, calling, invoking us to follow
Who will be the victor?
Will "self" reign?
Will we succumb to temptation?
Or will we remain strong in the Lord?
For the world calls

It is within our eyes view enticing us to enter
A battle for our mind to distract us away from God
To lead us down a wrong path
Our mouths are open to partake
Who will overcome? The world or God above?
There is a choice to be made
The battle is on! The struggle has begun!
Who will be the victor in your heart and mind?
But there is One who has already overcome!
Christ Jesus, the Lord over all!
For He reigns as the ruler victorious over Satan
And over the world, temptation and what so easily captures us
With His Holy Spirit power, we also can be over-comers!
Draw close to Him and He will draw close to you
God's Spirit will empower you and give you strength
He will cause you to rise above the struggle
Giving you fortitude to face temptation
To walk in newness of life in spite of your circumstances
For God is Mighty!
With God all things are possible!
He loves his children promising to strengthen and uphold them
With God, we can live victoriously!
When we are engaged in the battle!

Scriptures:

- Exodus 14:13-14 – "stand firm and you will see the deliverance the LORD will bring…the LORD will fight for you; you need only to be still."

- II Chronicles 20:1-30 – do not be afraid or discouraged… for the battle is not yours, but God's…stand firm and see the deliverance the LORD will give you,…have faith in the LORD your God and you will be upheld;…

- Psalm 144:1-2 – Praise be to the LORD my Rock, who trains

my hands for war, my fingers for battle. He is…my stronghold and my deliverer,…

- I Corinthians 10:11-13 – No temptation has seized you except what is common to man. And God is faithful…he will also provide a way out so that you can stand up under it.
- I Corinthians 15:56-58 – but thanks be to God! He gives us the victory through our Lord Jesus Christ…stand firm, let nothing move you.
- I Peter 5:6-11 – your enemy the devil prowls around like a roaring lion looking for someone to devour. Resist him, standing firm in the faith,…
- I John 4:4-6 - …the one who is in you is greater than the one who is in the world.

Thanks be to Christ for He has already won "the battle".

The Mighty Oak

It stands alone against the deep blue sky.
The mighty oak!
Gigantic with long outstretched branches rising skyward
Spreading out in all directions
Twisted and gnarled limbs touching the ground
Its massive trunk thickened with many years of growth
The ground completely shaded in dark shadows
The foliage dense overhead
A lifetime of experiences and people
Passing by unnoticed by the stately tree
Weathering the seasons for over two hundred years
The ground littered with fallen leaves and debris
Remnant acorns upon the ground, leftovers of a squirrel's dinner
What could topple such a tree?
Neither wind nor storm for it stands secure year after year
With roots running deep and spreading outward
A reminder of God's abiding love
His faithfulness to all generations!
The oak an expression of His might and power!

Oh, that our lives would be a reflection of the Mighty Oak
Exemplifying its very nature
Being securely rooted and grounded, "In Christ"
Jesus, the bedrock of our faith
Standing steadfast in what we believe
Planted deep and growing year upon year
In the Light of God's Word day by day
Receiving sustenance and nutrients, wisdom and truth
Richly feasting on the Word of God
Applying learned lessons
Being transformed and conformed to His image

Becoming a servant of the Lord
Stretching out in all directions to those in need
With outstretched arms of love and compassion
Feeding others with the gospel message
Blanketing them in love and prayer
Nurturing them in the Way!
And henceforth…when the storms of life come
The winds of discouragement, change, heartache and pain
Standing firm by God's enabling power
In the wake of turmoil and trouble
To be unwavering in our faith
Reliant upon God for His sufficient grace to see us through
At rest "in Christ" and His abiding love for us
For He is faithful!
He will hold us secure by His might and power
He is our "Mighty Oak"!
The Author and Perfecter of our faith
God Most High! Sovereign and Ruler over all!

Scriptures:

- Joshua 1:6-9 – "Be strong and courageous. Do not be terrified; do not be discouraged, for the LORD your God will be with you wherever you go."

- Psalm 1 All - …Blessed is the man…his delight is in the law of the LORD,…He is like a tree planted by streams of water,…

- Psalm 57 All – v.7- My heart is steadfast, O God, my heart is steadfast; I will sing and make music.

- Romans 4:18-5:5 - …Abraham…did not waver through unbelief…being fully persuaded that God had power to do what he had promised. …through our Lord Jesus Christ, through whom we have gained access by faith into this grace in which we now stand.

- EPHESIANS 1:3-14 - Spiritual blessings "in Christ"
- EPHESIANS 3:14-21 – …being rooted and established in love, … to grasp how wide and long and high and deep is the love of Christ,…
- EPHESIANS 6:10-18 - …be strong in the Lord and in his mighty power…so that when the day of evil comes, you may be able to stand your ground, and after you have done everything, to stand.
- HEBREWS 12:2 – Let us fix our eyes on Jesus, the author and perfecter of our faith,…
- I PETER 5:6-11 - …standing firm in the faith…And the God of all grace,…will himself restore you and make you strong, firm and steadfast. To him be the power for ever and ever. Amen.

Endeavoring to stand firm in Christ, my Savior!

The Rock

They stand tall and stately
Regal in splendor
Rising from the valley and lakes below
Thrusting forth against the blue sky
Towering above
Strong and immovable
Solid – Stable
With hard granite cliffs
Faces of impenetrable rock
Crevices marring the surface
Places where snow and vegetation collect
Changing according to seasons
Trees dotting the upper elevations
Poking into the sky overhead
Altered in appearance by the rising sun
Aglow in sunset's reflection
Majestic and supremely overwhelming
Mountains standing in grandeur
In regal splendor
Displaying God's Creation
The mountains declare the glory of the Lord!

What looms like a mountain before your eyes?
Impenetrable! Inescapable!
Encroaching into every facet of your day!
Insurmountable! Overwhelming!
So many things intrude into our lives.
Happenings that we have no control over
Hard circumstances
Causing us to worry and fret
Bringing uncertainty

Heartache and pain
A gigantic mountain looming before us
Life's strongholds of suffering and hardship
What do we do with them?
How do we scale these mountains?
How do we rise victorious above them?

By giving them to
The One who is higher than all!
"The Rock"
Christ Jesus, the strong and mighty One!
Who overrules in all areas of our lives.
Who is solid and stable
Steady and unchanging
The One we can depend upon above all else.
The Sovereign One!
Who rules supreme over all Creation
Our Rock!
Our Savior and Redeemer!
The One we can go to in prayer.
Who bears our every heartache, suffering and pain
Who loves us! Cares for us!
His Holy Spirit intercedes for us to the Father above
Christ is our Rock!
May He be glorified forever!

Scriptures:

- Psalm 19:14 – May the words of my mouth and the meditation of my heart be pleasing in your sight, O LORD, my Rock and my Redeemer.

- Psalm 40:1-5 - …he set my feet on a rock and gave me a firm place to stand.

- PSALM 46 ALL – v.1 – God is our refuge and strength, an ever-present help in trouble.
- ISAIAH 8:14, 28:16; ROMANS 9:33 – So this is what the Sovereign LORD says: "See, I lay a stone in Zion, a tested stone, a precious cornerstone for a sure foundation; the one who trusts will never be dismayed."
- ROMANS 8:26-27 - …the Spirit himself intercedes for us with groans that words cannot express.
- II CORINTHIANS 10:3-6 - …they (we) have a divine power to demolish strongholds.

Standing on the Rock of my salvation!

Chapter 8
God's Wondrous Care and Enabling Hand

PSALM 91 – ALL – He who dwells in the shelter of the Most High will rest in the shadow of the Almighty. …He will cover you with his feathers, and under his wings you will find refuge; his faithfulness will be your shield and rampart. "…Because he loves me," says the LORD, "I will rescue him; I will protect him, for he acknowledges my name."

Preface

There is great benefit to being a child of God! We rest within His constant care, loved by the Father and as His child we are cared for by God, protected and enabled by Him. God loves us and desires that we thrive and prosper in this life, bringing glory and honor to His Name. We are His ambassadors to the world; witnesses to God's wondrous care and enabling hand upon our life.

When difficulties and uncertainties come your way, what do you do? Like most people, we struggle through them unsure of the outcome. But with God…He is able to sustain you through life and beyond to eternal life with Him.

There are three ways that God cares for us and enables us to live our lives victoriously. First…there is God's Word. God has given His Word to teach us, rebuke, correct and train us in righteousness so that we are thoroughly equipped for every good work (II Timothy 3:16-17). God's Word is invaluable as we walk daily in this world and it is part of God's way to care for us and enable us in our daily life. However…we are to read it! It is of no value sitting on a shelf.

The second way God cares for us is through the power of His Holy Spirit for His Spirit comforts us in difficult times and counsels us when we are unsure of which way to go. What is so wonderful about God's Spirit is that He never leaves or forsakes us no matter the circumstance. God is ever present with us in His Spirit caring for us and enabling us to do and say what is pleasing to Him.

Lastly, God cares for us through the love and encouragement of other Christians as we live the life that God has given to us. Sometimes, we as humans, need the touch of a friend; a person to come alongside when we are distressed and discouraged. The church is God's way of caring and helping the community of His believers. What love the Father has for His children as He daily cares for us in so many ways and enables us to follow His leading in order to bring Him honor and glory.

Wondrous Care

The mockingbirds have been busy!
You can hear their song even before dawn's breaking
Waking you from slumber
Their chatter, their announcement to the day
Their song never the same, varied in melody
Diligent in their nest-building
Scavenging and gathering twigs, string and leaves
Intently intertwining them with soft downy feathers
Methodically fashioned over time, into a cozy secure nest
A haven for the next generation of baby mockingbirds
And once the nest is fashioned and the tiny eggs snuggly within
The vigil begins
The guarding and watching over those precious eggs
Mom… patiently protecting and warming
Dad… dive-bombing every threat that comes close
Mercilessly pecking upon the cat just walking by on the sidewalk
Attacking large black menacing crows in midair flight
Distracting prey away from the nest
Later, the process of feeding the tiny newborns
An endless back and forth, flitting across the lawn
Searching deep for worms, bugs and delectable tidbits
Finally, the day of needful flying instructions
Sending the fledglings out upon the wind currents of flight
Miracle in process! Wondrous care!

Can you not see God's hand upon the landscape?
His care over the birds of the air and His beautiful Creation!
His gentle and faithful concern for nature and His creatures
His love for all that surrounds us
But most especially…His care for us!
For the Lord loves us with an everlasting love.

He is not willing that any should perish
Once we belong to Him we rest secure in His love
Nothing can snatch us out of His hand
Nothing!
We dwell safe within His loving arms.
No matter the threats that surround us in life
The daily challenges and concerns; hurts and heartache
The persistent obstacles of life that threaten our peace
We rest cozy and secure within God's love and tender care
Nurtured by God's Holy Spirit
Guarded and surrounded by His army of angels
Fed daily by His living Word
Encouraged and built up in faith day upon day
Maturing and growing
Always within the Father's grasp and care
Becoming what He desires us to be
Sent out as His ambassadors to a hurting world
To spread the Good News of the Gospel of Christ
To walk in grace following in the Lord's footsteps
We are a miracle in process nurtured by a loving Father
Oh, that we would have a heart of thanksgiving!
A heart to praise Almighty God on high!
To look to Him in awe and wonder
To thank Him for His wondrous care!

Scriptures:

- DEUTERONOMY 33:26-29 – "There is no one like the God of Jeshurun, who rides on the heavens to help you and on the clouds in majesty. The eternal God is your refuge, and underneath are the everlasting arms.

- PSALM 8 ALL – v.4 - …what is man that you are mindful of him, the son of man that you care for him?

- PSALM 136 ALL - Give thanks to the LORD, for he is good…

who gives food to every creature. His love endures forever.
- PROVERBS 18:10 – The name of the LORD is a strong tower; the righteous run to it and are safe.
- NAHUM 1:7 – The LORD is good, a refuge in times of trouble. He cares for those who trust in him…
- MATTHEW 6:25-34 – Look at the birds of the air; they do not sow or reap or store away in barns, and yet your heavenly Father feeds them. Are you not much more valuable than they?
- JOHN 10:25-30 – "My Father, who has given them to me, is greater than all; no one can snatch them out of my Father's hand.
- EPHESIANS 5:1-2 – Be imitators of God, therefore, as dearly loved children and live a life of love, just as Christ loved us and gave himself up for us as a fragrant offering and sacrifice to God.

Resting secure in God's wondrous care!

At Rope's End

The view is indescribable
Surrounded by majestic mountains on all sides
Snow covered peaks
Lush green valleys in the distance
A panoramic landscape
Sheer cliffs with walls of weathered granite and rock
Up close and personal
A dangerous precipice, hanging in thin air
Clinging, life in the balance
A steep drop downward to jagged rocks below
Held fast by a strong grip
Spiked boots and a safety rope from above.
But…what if you were at rope's end?
Holding on by a thread with no safety net?
Doomed for disaster on the edge of falling?
Crushing rocks below and ultimate death
Would you be looking at the view?
Would you be concentrated on the scenery?

We all are at rope's end from time to time.
The end of a marriage perhaps alone and hurting
The end of a job holding promise and a future
The end of a life-long friendship
Lost in misunderstanding and conflict
Family relationships caught in bitterness and arguments
The end of financial security eaten away by debt and bills
The loss of a home taken away in foreclosure
Raising children through difficulties;
Not knowing which way to turn
How to help them, questions as to the future
The loss of a spouse replaced by quiet and loneliness

Health gone, sickness and pain instead
Hardship and suffering with no hope
At rope's end!
But…have we lost our sight of our security?
The One who holds the rope from above?
The One, who has a safety net below
We are secure in His loving arms!

Where is our focus?
On the scenery?
On the conflict and turmoil?
For at rope's end
We are most certainly safe and secure.
No matter what the circumstance
God holds us in His righteous right hand.
He will set our feet on a rock.
Giving us a firm place to stand
He will never leave us nor forsake us.
He remains forever faithful and true.
We are held fast and kept secure for eternity.
In His loving arms
Nothing can separate us from the love of Jesus.
He is steadfast and unchanging
He will not let go.
We are firmly in His grasp and care.
At rope's end!

Scriptures:

- Psalm 40:1-3 - …he set my feet on a rock and gave me a firm place to stand.

- Psalm 68:19-20 – Our God is a God who saves;…

- Psalm 73:21-28 - …you hold me by my right hand … God is the strength of my heart and my portion forever.

- PROVERBS 11:8 – The righteous man is rescued from trouble,…
- PROVERBS 29:25 - …whoever trusts in the Lord is kept safe.
- JOHN 17:6-18 - …I protected them and kept them safe by that name you gave me.
- ROMANS 8:35-39 - (Nothing)…will be able to separate us from the love of God that is in Christ Jesus our Lord.

Loved by God and kept safe within His care.

Blanketed

The mountains rise sharply from the valley floor
Strong and solid
Rising ever skyward, visible below
Blanketed on top
Covered with puffy white billowy clouds
Like whipped chiffon atop a luscious pie
Covering the mountain peaks
Hiding the details of the upper rock face
Soft and securely surrounded and encapsulated
Blanketed!
Not unlike a small infant wrapped in soft velour
Held secure within the folds
Warm and cuddly
Loved and protected
All extremities hidden within
Resting, asleep in slumber
Blanketed in the arms of God!
To feel so secure and loved!
Enveloped and at rest
Hidden
And yet there is a place where we can be
Blanketed in love!
Protected by strong arms, covered and hidden away
Loved beyond measure
Held securely for eternity
At rest
A place where the world is cast aside
A place beyond measure
That place is in the arms of Jesus!
Blanketed within the folds of His love
Surrounded by His peace and loving care

Held securely for all time!

But there are times…
When we slip out from within the folds
Escaping His grasp to go our own way
Leaving the security and warmth
Of God's embrace
Abandoning the safety of His love and protection
Thinking we know better
To live in disobedience and self-assertion
Oh, that we would choose to return
To humbly repent
Seeking once again reunion with the Father
Who is desirous of us!
To remain within the folds of His love and care
Covered by the blood of Jesus, His beloved Son
Forgiven
Resting securely in His saving grace
Blanketed in the arms of God!

SCRIPTURES:

- PSALM 104 ALL – v.1-2 – O LORD my God, you are great; you are clothed with splendor and majesty. He wraps himself in light as with a garment; he stretches out the heavens like a tent…

- PSALM 125:1-2 – As the mountains surround Jerusalem, so the LORD surrounds his people both now and forevermore.

- PROVERBS 14:26 – He who fears the LORD has a secure fortress, and for his children it will be a refuge.

- SONG OF SOLOMON 2:16-3:4 - …when I found the one my heart loves. I held him and would not let him go…

- Isaiah 38:15-20 – In your love you kept me from the pit of destruction; you have put all my sins behind your back.
- Romans 4:7-8 – "Blessed are they whose transgressions are forgiven, whose sins are covered. Blessed is the man whose sin the Lord will never count against him."
- II Peter 3:17-18 - …be on your guard so that you may not be carried away by the error of lawless men and fall from your secure position. But grow in the grace and knowledge of our Lord and Savior Jesus Christ. To him be glory both now and forever! Amen.

Blanketed in God's love and care!

BEAR CARE

Winter deep in slumber
Snow piled high upon the frozen ground
A silence in the air, an eerie stillness
Oak trees barren of foliage
Evergreens, dark and forest green
A harshness to the landscape
But deep within a darkened cave
Quiet life abounds
New birth
In the starkness of winter cold
Two small and defenseless bear cubs come to life
Blind at birth
Cuddled softly within the mother bear's thick coat
A new generation of tiny baby bears
Safe and protected
While the cold of winter rages outside
Surrounded by a mother bear's love and strength
Growing steadily, warm and safe within their cocoon
Finally spring's awakening!
Emerging to the new outside world
Small cubs remaining close-by
Taught and nurtured by their mother's protective love
Ever growing into adulthood
Thriving and maturing
Becoming what they were meant to be!

Do you ever feel like you are in the dead of winter?
In the grip of aloneness, heartache and circumstances
No one to whom you can talk about it
No one who even cares to listen
The storms of life raging all around

A winter chill
Friends off doing their own thing
Family members caught up in their own lives
And rightly so!

But…leaving you with a sense of helplessness
A feeling that no one truly loves you
No one cares. Not really!

Hey! Wait a minute!
Are we having thoughts of abandonment?
That no one cares? Really?
Of course they do!
You just don't "feel" like they do.
Remember, above all else
God is there! Always!
Every minute of every day!
He will never leave you nor forsake you!
He will wrap you in His strong capable arms.
He will keep you safe and warm through life's storms.
He is our Jehovah-Jireh, our Provider.
We are kept in His loving care.
Protected by His mighty hand
Enabled with His strength and power
We are taught and matured by His holy Word
Dependent and led by His Holy Spirit
Guiding us each step of the way
He causes us to thrive in His presence
To become what He purposed and planned us to be
And He has provided an eternal home for us
In His holy presence forevermore
Rest within His "bear care"
Lean on Christ, your Maker and Defender
He is your Gracious Savior.
Your risen and Glorious King!

Scriptures:

- **Deuteronomy 7:9** –Know therefore that the Lord your God is God; he is the faithful God, keeping his covenant of love to a thousand generations of those who love him and keep his commands.

- **Psalm 55:22; I Peter 5:7** – Cast your cares on the Lord and he will sustain you; he will never let the righteous fall.

- **Psalm 145 All** - …The Lord upholds all those who fall and lifts up all who are bowed down…The Lord is near to all who call on him,…

- **Daniel 7:1-18** - …one like a son of man, coming with the clouds of heaven…the saints of the Most High will receive the kingdom and will possess it forever--…

- **Ephesians 1:18-20** – I pray…that you may know…his incomparably great power for us who believe.

Resting within God's care

Illuminated by God's Light

A single silken strand
A delicate thread
Suspended in thin air
Traveling gently downward from tree to ground
Over ten feet in length
Cobweb's first beginning
With strength unseen
Unhindered by the gentle breeze
Sticky and entangling
Clinging to whatever it touches.
A spider's transport through space
Spun with diligence
Nearly invisible
Caught in the early rays of morning sunshine
Glistening, sparkling
Illuminated by God's Light!

God's Word
To many His Word is insignificant of little worth
Its truth irrelevant and unimportant
Of unseen value for living
Debated and misunderstood.
But it continues to shine forth
Giving strength and hope
Its origin stems from before creation
Yet pertinent for today's living
To those who read it
With heartfelt embrace
It captures men's hearts empowering our very life
Surrounding us with salvation's message
Fortifying us to live each day victoriously
Every precept, every principle and command
Teaches us!

Guides us!
Leads us!
In the ways of God
Showing us Who He is!
Revealing His might and glory
Opening up our view of
Who Jesus is…
Our Maker, Redeemer and Friend
Making known
The presence of the Holy Spirit
Leading us daily through the difficulties of life
God's Holy Word
The single most life-changing book of all time
The Bible
Steady and unchanging
God's very words to us in a dark world
Illuminated by God's Light!

Why would we not read it?

Scriptures:

- Deuteronomy 8:3 - …man does not live on bread alone but on every word that comes from the mouth of the LORD.

- Psalm 119:9-16 - …I have hidden your word in my heart that I might not sin against you.

- Proverbs 1:1-7, 2:1-11 and 3:1-6 – The benefits of attaining Wisdom.

- II Timothy 3:14-17 - …All Scripture is God-breathed and is useful for teaching, rebuking, correcting and training in righteousness, …

- Hebrews 4:12-13 – For the word of God is living and active. Sharper than any double-edged sword,…

Clinging to God's Word every day in every way!

Restoration

A summer of neglect! The garden is a mess!
The roses need mulching and fertilizing
Trimming out the dead and dried up blossoms
The ground cover is overgrown
The flower beds have weeds of all different varieties
Old plants need pulling, new plants need to be planted for fall
Trees and bushes trimmed
Old dried-up fruit picked up off the ground
And the list goes on and on and on!
To look upon all the chores needing to be done
A seemingly insurmountable task
However…Do-able!
Step by step, one task at a time, day by day
Achieving what the Lord desires me to do for this day!
Appreciating God's natural splendor in the garden
Taking courage and getting to work
Achieving it bit by bit
Being grateful and thankful at the results
Looking forward with anticipation
A harvest of great worth! A garden restored in beauty!

Doesn't God want to do the same for us?
Restore us in beauty before the throne of grace!
Even when we have been neglectful leaving the path of His will
When we are lost in sin; walking away
Our spiritual life dried-up and dead overgrown with weeds
Needing to purge our lives of what is displeasing to the Lord
Confessing our sin and neglect
Returning to the Lord with a whole heart in repentance
Receiving God's forgiveness and grace
But oft-times we look upon our lives with contempt and disgust

Feeling unworthy of God's saving touch
Beyond His forgiveness and love
Having a fatalistic attitude
With an inability to change and come to Him
But God is love!
There is "no one" beyond His grace and ability to restore.
He has provided a Way toward restoration!
Christ Jesus, the Savior of our soul!
Take courage!
Christ has achieved for us salvation and reconciliation.
He has restored us by His death upon the Cross!
And able to restore the years that the locust have eaten!
All the past is covered by His atoning sacrifice.
"It is finished!"
When He shed His precious blood for us!
We are cleansed, forgiven and made righteous in His eyes!
Restored! Able to walk in newness of life!
Restored to fellowship and in rightness with the Father
Oh, that we would have a grateful heart.
Thankful for the new life we have been given
Looking with anticipation for Christ's return
Life eternally with the Father
For we are restored and beautiful in His eyes!

SCRIPTURES:

- PSALM 51:1-12 – …Create in me a pure heart, O God,…restore to me the joy of your salvation and grant me a willing spirit, to sustain me.

- JOEL 2:25-32 – "I will repay you for the years the locusts have eaten…I am the LORD your God…and everyone who calls on the name of the LORD will be saved;…

- JOHN 19:28-30 – …Jesus said, "It is finished." With that, he bowed his head and gave up his spirit.

- ROMANS 5:8-11 – But God demonstrates his own love for us in this: While we were still sinners, Christ died for us…we have now received reconciliation.
- II CORINTHIANS 5:16-21 - …Therefore, if anyone is in Christ, he is a new creation;…Be reconciled to God. God made him who had no sin to be sin for us, so that in him we might become the righteousness of God.
- EPHESIANS 1:3-14 - …In him we have redemption through his blood, the forgiveness of sins, in accordance with the riches of God's grace…
- I PETER 5:6-11 - …And the God of all grace, who called you to his eternal glory in Christ,…will himself restore you and make you strong, firm and steadfast. To him be the power for ever and ever. Amen.

Thankful that Christ has restored me to new life in Him

The Small Stuff

The sprinklers swooshing back and forth on the lawn
Watery spray filtering through the air
Clinging to the evergreen cypress branches
Heavy with moisture
Covering the dense foliage
A tiny green hummingbird
Dousing himself in droplets of cool water
Taking his early morning bath
Fluttering
Preening himself
Shaking off the excess
Darting here and there
Fluffing his feathers
You could almost have missed him
Hidden amongst the greenery
Small and obscure
A small part of God's wondrous creation!

A sunny afternoon
Bright sun and warmth
Flowers in full bloom
A small humble bumblebee
Shiny black and laden with yellow pollen
Traveling, here and there, amid the blossoms
From one flower to the next
And then off
Gone, returning to the hive
Small and obscure
God's delicate creation on display!

Does not God care for the details in my life?
The small stuff!
Like the hummingbird and the bumblebee
Does He not care so much more for even ME!
For the concerns of my every day?
The hurts in my heart?
The troubles that come my way?
Difficulties and strains of life?
The menial tasks that must be done?
The "what's-for-dinner" question?
What clothes will I wear?
The bills, the laundry?
All the small stuff, the details in every day?
If God cares for the hummingbird and the bumblebee
How much more does He care for me?

The small things in our lives
Are within His loving care
We need not worry or fret
We can safely leave them there.
For God cares for us!
We can depend upon Him
He loves us without reservation
We are kept within His loving arms
Trust that He will supply your every need
For He truly is a "Great God" indeed!
And He is able to take care of the small stuff!

Scriptures:

- DEUTERONOMY 29:29 – The secret things belong to the LORD our God, but the things revealed belong to us and to our children,…

- PSALM 55:22 – Cast your cares on the LORD and he will sustain you; he will never let the righteous fall.
- MATTHEW 5:25-34 - …Look at the birds of the air; they do not sow or reap or store away in barns, and yet your heavenly Father feeds them. Are you not much more valuable than they?"
- PHILIPPIANS 4:19 – And my God will meet all your needs according to his glorious riches in Christ Jesus.

Thanking God for His daily care.

"Look Up!"

Deep within the canyon walls
Advancing on foot slowly along the shallow stream's path
Water rushing swiftly underfoot
Swirling along the riverbed in eddies
Shifting the pebbles in its wake
Turning muddy when agitated by one's footfall
Cliffs gradually closing inward
Sandstone of brilliant red and orange
Swirled and grooved by time
Sculptured with design
Eroded by wind and water
Adjacent side-walls rising steeply upward
With crevices catching the light
Deepening shadows
Hemmed in by the encroaching canyon
Ever-narrowing with each step
The water-filled streambed reaching from side to side
No way of escape
But "look up"!
The deep blue of God's brilliant sky shines from above!
Illuminating the canyon with shafts of radiant light!

Feel like you are in a canyon sometimes?
Encroached upon on every side
Hemmed in by circumstances
Besieged by difficulties with no way of escape
Buffeted
Swirling and shifting along in life
With no sense of direction and not sure of your footing
In the shadows
Losing sight of what is important and lasting

Stop! Look up!
Don't look at the encroaching walls and swirling waters
God is faithful!
Are you caught in the temptation to doubt Him?
He will provide a way out, a way of escape!
He will give you a firm place to stand
Even in the midst of your canyon
For God's light shines from above!
He is the Light in the darkness!
Shining through to you wherever you may be
God's Word is a lamp and a light
Giving direction to your pathway
Leading you through the canyons of life
God is our place of refuge
Our Deliverer!
When troubles surround you like mighty waters
He surrounds you with His love and protection
With His care and provision
Able to help you when you've lost your way
Look to Him!
Fix your eyes on the Lord
For He is your salvation
He is your Jehovah Jireh, your Provider!
The Mighty One!
Look up!

Scriptures:

- GENESIS 22:1-18 – v.14 – So Abraham called that place The LORD Will Provide. And to this day it is said, "On the mountain of the LORD it will be provided."

- PSALM 32:6-11 – v.7 – You are my hiding place; you will protect me from trouble and surround me with songs of deliverance. Selah

- PSALM 119:105 – Your word is a lamp to my feet and a light for my path.
- JOHN 1:29-34 - … "Look, the Lamb of God, who takes away the sin of the world!"
- JOHN 8:12, 12:35-36 - "I am the light of the world. Whoever follows me will never walk in darkness, but will have the light of life."
- I CORINTHIANS 10:12-13 - …God is faithful; …he will also provide a way out so that you can stand up under it.
- HEBREWS 3:1-6 – Therefore, holy brothers, who share in the heavenly calling, fix your thoughts on Jesus, the apostle and high priest whom we confess…Christ is faithful…

Clinging to Christ, looking to Him in the canyons of life!

Dormant Trees

They stand stark against the winter sky
Limbs barren and devoid of foliage
Standing alone against the elements
Unfazed by the wind and the rain
With twisted and gnarled bark
Every flaw visible, each tiny branch exposed
Dead twigs falling to the ground
Not a leaf in sight
Hoping for an early spring to arrive
Patiently awaiting the warmth of the sun's rays
For longer days and growth to begin
Leaves and greenery to appear
Spring's rebirth
An awakening from a long winter's sleep
But in the meantime standing firm
Solid and unmovable
Securely planted
Waiting for God's timing to come alive
Dormant trees!

Do you feel like a dormant tree?
In the midst of winter; barren and alone
Bombarded by the elements
The circumstances of life
Feeling vulnerable and exposed
Devoid of friends or people to come to your aid
Hurt and lost
In a sea of heartache and pain
Hoping that this crisis will be over soon
Waiting for a new day to come forth
Things to improve

For spring to arrive in your life
Take courage! Stand firm!
All is not lost!
God is still sovereign and in control!
He will sustain you!
He will cause you to stand secure in your faith.
For he is the "Rock" of your salvation!
Solid, Unmovable
You are securely planted "in Him".
Remain in His love
A new day is dawning!
He will see you through the struggle
Bringing you out in victory and with great joy
To the place that he desires you to reside
Leafing out!
Transformed and changed to reflect His character
All according to His plan and purpose
So stand firm!
Wait for God's perfect timing
Rest in Him!
Call upon His name and seek His face
He will surely save and rescue you!
For he is God!
Nothing is impossible with Him!
You will not remain as a dormant tree.
You shall be changed!
Growing, coming forth, secure in His loving arms!

Scriptures:

- Psalm 91 All – He who dwells in the shelter of the most high will rest in the shadow of the almighty. ... "because he loves me," says the LORD, "I will rescue him; I will protect him,...I will be with him in trouble, I will deliver him and honor him.

With long life will I satisfy him and show him my salvation."
- Proverbs 4:18-27 – The path of the righteous is like the first gleam of dawn, shining ever brighter till the full light of day. … let your eyes look straight ahead, fix your gaze directly before you.
- Isaiah 26:3-4 – all - …the LORD, is the rock eternal.
- II Corinthians 3:18 – and we, who with unveiled faces all reflect the LORD's glory, are being transformed into his likeness with ever-increasing glory, which comes from the LORD, who is the spirit.
- Ephesians 6:10-18 - …therefore put on the full armor of God, so that when the day of evil comes, you may be able to stand your ground, and after you have done everything, to stand.

**Standing firm! Trusting and waiting!
Thanking God in the meantime!**

Perfection's Best

The first garden; God's wondrous creation!
Perfect in every way as God is perfect
Beauty personified in the Garden of Eden
The ideal locale wherein man was to dwell forever
But in place of the ideal
God's sublime plan for mankind
Perfection was lost!
Sin entered the world amid God's perfect garden
And yet…in today's realm of horticulture
Man seeks to recreate that which God did perfectly.
"The perfect garden"
Well trimmed trees and manicured bushes
Weed-free flower beds! No dandelions!
Vibrant, full blooming flowers year round
Trimmed and luscious green lawns
Fruitful trees and bountiful vegetables, flawless and delicious
We endeavor to make perfect…that which is not!
Striving always for perfection
A pristine garden!

And so the striving continues beyond the garden
Into each and every life, a striving to be "in control"
Seeking perfection
To have everything well ordered and in its place
A well trimmed life!
Weed-free of difficulties, pain and hardship
Everything wonderful and flowery! No dandelions!
Only success and goodness allowed
Fruitfulness and prosperity
Always "in control" of the outcome
Striving to figure out the "what ifs" in life

Blowing every difficulty out of proportion
Planning for every contingence and scenario
Seeking only our own agenda and outcome
Having all our ducks in a straight line
Stressed out if we don't have instant answers
And yet…inescapable non-perfection!
Things go wrong!
The weeds of life persist and the flaws of mankind remain
Perfection is lost! Life happens!
Not all is perfection and loveliness.
We endeavor to make perfect that which is not!

To whom can we turn?
There is but One who can fill our deepest need.
Let us run to the One who is perfect!
To God who is infinite wisdom and understanding
Whose plans are perfect in every way!
To a Savior who upholds us and loves us unconditionally
Who can change our striving into trusting!
Change our messes into marvelous masterpieces
The only One who can gird us with His perfection
And bring us into everlasting life in glory!
Perfection's best!

SCRIPTURES:

- PROVERBS 3:1-10 – …Trust in the LORD with all your heart and lean not on your own understanding; in all your ways acknowledge him, and he will make your paths straight.

- ISAIAH 43:16-21 – "Forget the former things;…I am doing a new thing!…I am making a way in the desert and streams in the wasteland.

- MATTHEW 6:19-34 – … "For where your treasure is, there your heart will be also. … "Therefore, I tell you, do not worry about your life,…but seek first his kingdom and his righteousness, and all these things will be given to you as well."

- MATTHEW 7:13-14 - …But small is the gate and narrow the road that leads to life, and only a few find it.

- II CORINTHIANS 4:1-18 - …For our light and momentary troubles are achieving for us an eternal glory that far outweighs them all. So we fix our eyes not on what is seen, but on what is unseen. For what it seen is temporary, but what is unseen is eternal.

- HEBREWS 12:1-13 - …Let us fix our eyes on Jesus, the author and perfecter of our faith…consider him who endured such opposition from sinful men, so that you will not grow weary and lose heart.

Still learning to trust rather than finagle my own way

- Weeping Willow Waters -

Wispy weeping willow, gently wash o'er me,
      With your graceful limbs and lush green leaves;
Swaying calmly in the balmy breeze,
      A tree of daintiness and grace
      God's perfect peace displayed.

Watered by a rushing bubbling stream
      Alongside a peaceful shore;
Its thirsty roots reaching ever outward
      To grasp clear water, more and more
      God's perfect provision provided.

Fast growing, the weeping willow thrives and grows
      With branches broad and wide;
Spreading, drooping to the ground,
      Cool shade within, it does provide…
      God's perfect protection assured.

From shoreline soil, nourishment is found;
      Lush green foliage coming forth;
Taking what the humble earth doth provide
      God turns it into growth…
      God's perfect transformation exhibited.

Through winter's cold and dormant stage,
      The weeping willow sleeps quite sound;
But returns vibrantly back to life,
      When warming spring comes round…
      God's perfect restoration supplied.

Earth's weeping willow is a reflection of our lives,
> Tapped into God's provision for its life
And as it takes from water, soil and air,
> God gives it peace and calm, life without strife…
> God is the source of all life.

May I be tapped into God's life-giving stream!
> Nurtured by His mighty Word
Listening to my Sovereign heavenly Father,
> Obeying what I've heard.
May I live a pure and clean, abundant life,
> Dependent upon God's love and grace;
And may I rest secure within His peace
> And daily seek Christ's radiant and loving face.

SCRIPTURE:

- GENESIS 2:9 – And the LORD God made all kinds of trees grow out of the ground—trees that were pleasing to the eye and good for food.
- PSALM 1:3 – He is like a tree planted by streams of water, which yields its fruit in season and whose leaf doe not wither. Whatever he does prospers.
- JEREMIAH 17:7-8 - …blessed is the man who trusts in the LORD, whose confidence is in him. He will be like a tree planted by the water that sends out its roots by the stream.
- EPHESIANS 3:14-21 - …rooted and established in love…the love of Christ.
- REVELATIONS 22:2, 16, 19 - …Christ is the Root.

Tapping into the source of life, Christ, my Lord

Sliver Moon

Sliver Moon…
There you are just above the horizon
        A mere thin wisp of a narrow slender crescent
Barely visible; a curved sliver
        Of your former glory and shape
Arched, shining mutely
        Against the setting sun's dusk in the afterglow of day
So hard to distinguish and yet
        So unmistakably there and strangely visible
Soon to set yourself along with
        The retreating orb of the day's sun
Sliver moon, how slender, small and insignificant
        Soon you will gracefully retreat from sight !

Sliver Moon…
Does anyone notice your presence and subtle beauty?
        Or are they too busy to mark your passing?
Fleeting, retreating and faintly obscure
        Invisible…where have you gone?
Oh, sliver moon!
        Like the passing out of view of a longtime friend
who moves far away.
        Or the loss and death of a loved one,
where only fond memories remain.
        Perhaps the absence of one's health,
a mere reflection of youth long since gone.
        Or…one's security, one's children, one's home
gone, fleeting from sight. Irretrievable!

And yet…
        Intact, whole, with potential to shine once more
We see in part the whole;
        In reality the whole exists apart from our sight

For where there is…
> Loss; God gives comfort.
> Death; God brings newness of life in Christ.
> No health…forbearance.
> No security…rest and dependency in Him.
> No family…you are God's child and totally loved.
> No earthly home…God provides an eternal place

Of rest in heaven

Sliver moon…
> A reminder of God's awesome glory

To see you full and glowing brightly,
> In brilliant iridescent splendor

In luster you shine; in wholeness you glow;
> From God's mercy and grace your beauty doth flow.

Scriptures:

- Deuteronomy 33:26-29 – "There is no one like the God of Jeshurun, who rides on the heavens to help you and on the clouds in his majesty. The eternal God is your refuge, and underneath are the everlasting arms.

- Psalm 8 All – O LORD, our Lord, how majestic is your name in all the earth! …When I consider your heavens, the work of your fingers, the moon and the stars, which you have set in place,…

- Psalm 74:16 – The day is yours, and yours also the night; you established the sun and moon.

- I Peter 5:10-11 – And the God of all grace,…will himself restore you and make you strong, firm and steadfast. To him be the power for ever and ever. Amen.

Observing God's healing and restoring grace

The Misty Lowlands

They go on seemingly forever!
Endlessly in all directions
The misty lowlands!
Trees and swamp—swamp and trees!
Densely shaded beneath the sun's rays
Only mere tiny shafts of light reaching the ground
Stagnant water and mossy rocks
Lichen growing on the northern side of trees
Decaying leaves
Eerie things filling the shadows hidden in the fog
Muddy hollows sucking down anything that passes by
Creatures in the night slithering and creeping
The hoot of a faraway distant owl
And the mist persists
Engulfing, filling every crevice of the air
Humid and oppressive
Depressing
But the bog and fog are not out of God's view
They exist within His created world
Under His sovereign realm and power
The misty lowlands!

Do you ever feel that you are there?
In the misty lowlands of life?
Surrounded by a swamp of despair and heartache
Not able to see the light of day
Sucked under with the cares of this world
Caught in the mire of life, lost in the fog
Oppressed and overwhelmed
By things out of your control
Filling your every waking hour

Creeping into the sleepless watches in the dark of night
Making your mind wander
Allowing fear and frustration to enter into your thoughts
Taking over and engulfing your life
Falling into depression and hopelessness
Held in Satan's grip
Don't go there!
Remember, you are not out of God's view!
You are under His sovereign realm, power and control.
You are precious to the Lord!
Your life is in His mighty hand!
Even when you feel like you are in…
The misty lowlands!

Moreover…
God has a plan and a purpose for your life!
And it is not to dwell in the misty lowlands of this world
You were made for realms on high!
Even in the midst of the mire of each day
God's desire is that you trust Him!
That you lean not on your own understanding
That you acknowledge Him in all your circumstances
He will make your paths straight.
He will cause you to stand secure in Him
He is the "Rock" on whom you can depend.
God Most High will sustain you!
In the misty lowlands!

SCRIPTURES:

- PSALM 18:25-36 - …It is God who arms me with strength and makes my way perfect. …your right hand sustains me;…
- PSALM 40 ALL – v.1-2 – I waited patiently for the LORD; he turned to me and heard my cry. He lifted me out of the slimy

pit, out of the mud and mire; he set my feet on a rock and gave me a firm place to stand.

- Psalm 71 All – v.20 – Though you have made me see troubles, many and bitter; you will restore my life again; from the depths of the earth you will again bring me up.
- Proverbs 3:5-6, 21-26 – Trust in the LORD with all your heart…he will make your paths straight…for the LORD will be your confidence…
- II Corinthians 4:7-18 – …We are hard pressed on every side… For our light and momentary troubles are achieving for us an eternal glory that far outweighs them all.

Trusting God in the misty lowlands of life

The View From the Boat

I don't like boats!
Probably due to extreme seasickness
But I've ventured on a couple in my lifetime
The view is spectacular out on the water!
Horizon to horizon
A vastness outstretched before your eyes
With wondrous sunrises and gorgeous dazzling sunsets
Dipping down into the depths of the water
The calm lapping of waves against the sides of the boat
The serenity and peacefulness
Dolphins running alongside a cruise liner
In the blue crystal-clear water
Tiny crests of whitecaps frosting the ocean
The view is wonderful!
But in the midst of a storm?
With clouds descending in a darkening sky
Waves buffeting the ship or boat
Swelling up, engulfing
Being tossed to and fro by the rising wind
Losing your bearing and all sense of direction
Unable to see the shoreline
Our view obscured
Causing us to have only one goal in mind
To make a beeline for safety and find calm serene waters
To reach safe harbor!

Isn't that human nature?
Safety and security
We flee from things that are difficult

Taxing situations, trying to escape
The arduous and painful, the tumultuous
Circumstances that toss us about engulfing our days
Causing us to lose our bearing
Obstructing our sense of direction
Preoccupying our time and efforts
Taking away our safety and security
We yearn for the easy way
The shoreline
A safe harbor of respite
But God calls us to enter the fray
Calls us to get in the boat
To enter deep water no matter the cost
Climb aboard! Follow me!
Go!
There is a risk!
But the view is spectacular!
Jesus resides within the boat!
There is no safer place to be because Jesus is there!
He is beside you! Always with you!
Upholding you!
He is your salvation; your safe harbor!
He will never leave you nor forsake you.
And the view to look upon his face
The wondrous Lord of all! Jesus!
Beautiful beyond any sunset
Dazzling in splendor, calm and serene
The prince of peace!
Gaze on him!
The view within the boat!

SCRIPTURES:

- PSALM 27:1-6 - the LORD is my light and my salvation—

whom shall I fear? ...one thing I ask of the LORD, ...to gaze upon the beauty of the LORD and to seek him in his temple.

- PSALM 91 ALL – he who dwells in the shelter of the Most High, will rest in the shadow of the Almighty. ..."because he loves me," says the LORD, "I will rescue him; I will protect him,...
- PSALM 105:1-4 - ...look to the LORD and his strength; seek his face always.
- MATTHEW 8:23-27, MARK 4:36-41, LUKE 8:22-25 - ...he got up and rebuked the wind and the waves, and it was completely calm.
- MATTHEW 16:24-28 – Then Jesus said to his disciples, "if anyone would come after me, he must deny himself and take up his cross and follow me.
- JAMES 1:2-8 - ...but when he asks, he must believe and not doubt, because he who doubts is like a wave of the sea, blown and tossed by the wind.

In the boat with Jesus!

Chapter 9
God's Call to the Believer

EPHESIANS 5:1-2 – Be imitators of God, therefore, as dearly loved children and live a life of love, just as Christ loved us and gave himself up for us as a fragrant offering and sacrifice to God.

EPHESIANS 5:8 – For you were once darkness, but now you are light in the Lord. Live as children of light.

Preface

Are you a child of God? Then…what has God called you to do? What is God calling you to become? Some people live a lifetime and never know what God is calling them to be. God ultimately is calling each one of us to Himself, to live with Him eternally in His presence. But…what are we to do in the meantime here on earth?

When Jesus called His disciples to follow Him and become fishers of men, He called them to a life other than what they were doing. They heard the call to follow and went. They learned from the Master and after Jesus was crucified and rose to glory, these same men were called to be witnesses and spread the gospel of Christ to all nations. That call is still the same today to every believer. We are Christ's emissaries to the world with the gospel of salvation.

However, in the process of being Christ's witnesses, we also are called to live out the Christian life by what we do and say in our everyday life. We are to be Christ-like, following in Christ's footsteps and endeavoring to emulate to the world what Christ would do. So what does it mean to be Christ-like? Paul gives us in many of his letters in the New Testament character qualities to pursue. We are to be a living sacrifice pleasing to God, seeking to love sincerely those around us. We also are to be joyful, patient and faithful in prayer. We should also be willing to share and be hospitable. Ephesians gives us guidelines on how to be imitators of God and live a life of love. There are so many verses in God's Word that tell us what God desires our life to look like becoming more and more like Jesus. This lifestyle is a call upon our life from God.

So…where should you start to heed the call of God upon your life becoming all that God desires you to be? Start at the beginning of your faith and step by step follow and obey the directions of God's Holy Spirit. God's call upon your life is an exciting adventure. Follow and obey for the road leads straight to God and into His presence. What better call to follow!

Almost Missed?

In the early morning light, the bush shook.
        The pink and white blossoms of the shrub vibrating
The small yellow-breasted sparrows hidden deep within
        Skipping from branch to branch
In search of tiny bugs and seeds for breakfast
        So secluded, barely visible…
                      …almost missed?

The glorious glow of the rising sun
        In vibrant pink colors covering the sky
God's start to a day of beginnings and possibilities
        Proclaiming His majesty and glory
Rolling over in bed for the sake of an additional snooze
        Albeit the glorious sunrise could be…
                      …almost missed?

The busyness of the day with demanding schedules
        Appointments to keep, chores to get done
Going this way and that, filling our day with nothingness
        Have we stopped to look at God's creation?
The beauty and the majesty of mountains and trees
        Proclaiming His presence or is all this…
                      …almost missed?

The day has been filled with work and duties galore
        The clamor of life and the trials of the day
Home at last! For some peace and quiet!
        Time for myself without any demands!
Or spending time to play with the children, talk to my wife
        The joy of togetherness and family time…
                      …almost missed?

There are so many needs and concerns in the world today
        In our immediate circle of friends and acquaintances
Time to visit a sick friend; to send a card to someone grieving;

    To share the Word of God, the gospel of Christ
Being part of the family of God with an open heart of love
    Opportunities for sincere concerns to be cared for…
        …almost missed?
There are not enough hours in the day
    How can you expect me to find time to pray?
Exhausted with the life that constantly draws me away
    No time to read God's Word today
Drawing near to God and learning of Him
    Spending a brief moment in sweet communion…
        …almost missed?
Death looms in the future down the path of life
    A certainty! Yet seemingly distant and ignored
Tomorrow I have plans. There's no need to think about it today.
    No need to come to Jesus, the Creator and Sustainer of life
There is still time to decide; do I really need Him now.
    Yet Jesus gently draws us to His side…
        …almost missed?
For a life with Christ brings His love and forgiveness.
    Eternal life with Him forever and joy unspeakable
A life of fulfillment with lasting reward, without waste or loss
    A life lived in the power of the Holy Spirit
To overcome the trials of life and live pleasing to the Lord
    A life with purpose and direction…
        …almost missed?
Don't miss Christ, whose life gives life to all who believe
    Don't miss the One who is all powerful and majestic
Don't miss a life filled with His beauty and salvation
    For to choose "not" to give your heart to Christ in faith,
To follow and love Him with your entire being…
    …is the most important "miss" of all!
        …almost missed?

Scriptures:

- John 3:16 – "For God so loved the world that he gave his one and only Son, that whoever believes in him shall not perish but have eternal life."
- John 6:35 – "I am the bread of life." – v. 51 – "the living bread"
- John 8:12 – "I am the light of the world"
- John 10:7-9 – "I am the gate for the sheep"
- John 10:14 – "I am the good shepherd"
- John 11:25-26 – Jesus said… "I am the resurrection and the life.
- John 14:6 – "I am the way and the truth and the life. No one comes to the Father except through me."
- John 15:1 – "I am the true vine"

So grateful that I belong to Christ and didn't "miss" Him!

Circles of Raindrops

The clouds are gathering overhead
The sky is darkening
A blackness creeping into the clouds
The denseness increasing
And one by one
The raindrops begin to fall
A few here and there casting circles upon quiet still waters
Round concentric orbs upon the crystal clear surface
Circles working their way outward
Ever widening
Growing
Touching other circles nearby
Delicately embracing each other
Intertwined together
More and more droplets
Gathering momentum
A joining together, an overlapping
Each circle encompassing the other
As the rain gathers in constant procession
Circles of raindrops!

And so the circles expand
Like the touching of one life to another
Each unique and unto themselves
Yet in the world
A part of mankind
Joined together by God's design
"It is not good for man to be alone," says the Lord.
And so we are not!
Each life a part of all the others
Whether, mother and father, brother, sister, son or daughter

Relatives and friends, co-workers and neighbors
Even more so in the family of God
Are we not all part of the body of Christ?
Unique and yet bound to one another
Christ as our common bond
Holding us together
In love and unity
Delicately embracing one another in the spirit of friendship
Intertwined in service
All doing their part
Growing in wisdom and knowledge
Embracing one another
Expanding in witness to a world in need
Or so it should be!
For…Christ calls us to fellowship!
To love one another because He first loved us
He calls us to the banquet table
As the bride of Christ
To fellowship with Him in the heavenly realms
In one accord
In love and unity together with Christ
Gathered in constant procession
Before the throne of Christ
To worship and adore Him forevermore!

Wherein lays your fellowship, your belonging, your hope?
Are you part of Christ's circle of Life?

Scriptures:

- **Genesis 2:18** – The LORD God said, "It is not good for the man to be alone. I will make a helper suitable for him."
- **Matthew 22:34-40; Mark 12:28-31** – … "Love the Lord your

God…love your neighbor as yourself."
- ROMANS 12:3-8 - …so in Christ we who are many form one body, and each member belongs to all the others.
- I CORINTHIANS 12:12-31 - …Now you are the body of Christ, and each one of you is a part of it.
- EPHESIANS 4:1-16 - … From him (Christ) the whole body, joined and held together by every supporting ligament, grows and builds itself up in love, as each part does its work.
- I JOHN 3:11-24 - …And this is his command: to believe in the name of his Son, Jesus Christ, and to love one another as he commanded us.
- REVELATION 19:1-10 - … 'Blessed are those who are invited to the wedding supper of the Lamb!'"

How precious are the saints in the body of Christ!

Earnestly Seeking

Summer is quickly passing
Hot weather giving way to cool nights, shortened days
Fall cleanup has arrived
The rose bushes need attentive care
Summer's heat has taken its toll
Dead leaves and branches amid each rosebush
Debris needing to be discarded
Thrown away
Suckers growing at the base
Cutting out required
Cultivation and fertilizer needed
Deep watering
There is still time!
Before winter's required trimming
Time for new growth
The goal is new blossoms for fall time
Desiring added bouquets of beauty
Beautiful flowers in abundance
Earnestly seeking!
God's transformation of weathered worn rose bushes
Into productive and blossoming plants of glorious flowers!

What do you strive to earnestly seek?
What is the motivation of your day?
How you live determines what you produce in life.
Life sometimes is a struggle
Like the summer heat
With debris in areas of our lives
Things that take up our time
Suckers sapping our strength
Drawing upon our thoughts and energy

Distracting, leading us astray
Cutting out is required
A discarding of those things not pleasing to God
Cultivation and fertilizer are needed
God's Word bringing guidance and direction
A purpose and plan to our life
Christ's Word leading to repentance and holiness
Salvation's song!
There is still time!
God is not willing that any should perish!
Gód's desire is that we bloom where He has planted us
Producing blossoms in abundance
Fruitfulness
Our lives becoming a beautiful bouquet
Of righteousness and love toward others
Earnestly seeking Him!
Being transformed by the renewing of our minds
Desiring to follow Him
To daily abide with Him
To bring Him praise and honor and glory!
Earnestly seeking!
Life eternal
In the presence of the Holy One!
Face to face forevermore!
How earnest is your seeking?

SCRIPTURES:

- I CHRONICLES 28:9-10 – If you seek him, he will be found by you.

- ISAIAH 35 ALL – The Joy of the Redeemed - …he will come to save you.

- ISAIAH 55 ALL – v.6 – Seek the LORD while he may be found; call on him while he is near.

- ROMANS 12:1-2 - …be transformed by the renewing of your mind. Then you will be able to test and approve what God's will is—his good, pleasing and perfect will.
- COLOSSIANS 1:9-14 - …live a life worthy of the Lord…bearing fruit in every good work, growing in the knowledge of God,…
- II PETER 3:8-13 – The Lord is…not wanting anyone to perish, but everyone to come to repentance.

Desiring to grow in God's grace and in the knowledge of Him

Reflections

Have you noticed the contrasts that earthly nature brings?
The opposites in God's creation and all created things
From night to day
Warming sun and cool moonlight
Hot and cold
Sunny days versus rainy storms unfold
Clear crisp skies but also cloudy gray
Contrasts exist in so many ways
The dazzling flowers amid the pesky weeds
Prickly cactus plants versus evergreen trees
Varieties, reflections of God's creation
Do you think our world reflects the original Garden of Eden?
Or
Is man a reflection of his own environment?
Following man's sinful nature, his own selfish fulfillment
For amid the world of good and bad contrasts do exist
A pursuit of God but also sin and worldliness
Man's self-seeking ways and selfishness
Reflecting his own sinful nature and ungodliness
Should man not reflect their Creator, the living God?
The One who loves them, their Sovereign Lord
Who reigns above!
Should we not believe the truth of God's Holy Word?
Rejecting Satan's lie
Pursuing true and noble qualities and daily on Him rely?
But the contrasts of this world bombard our every day
Causing us to wander from God's path, causing us to go astray
Will we not turn those hateful things?
The evil that we do
Into godliness and holiness, serving our Lord and living pure?

For
God above is holy
There is no one else like Him.
There is no contrast in His character
He is pure and good from within.
His Sovereignty rules over all.
He is loving and full of grace
He has compassion for the lost
And we're invited to meet Him face to face.
Would we not desire to love and follow Him?
Reflecting Him in all our ways
Or
Would we be ashamed to come before His mighty throne?
Would we, from His presence, be cast away?
Should we not be a reflection of His love and grace to us?
Showing mercy and generosity
To those around us, whom we touch?
For Christ's sacrifice for us was perfect in every way
Should we not reflect His love?
To those who come into our day?

Scriptures:

- Proverbs 27:19 – As water reflects a face, so a man's heart reflects the man.

- II Corinthians 3:18 – And we, who with unveiled faces all reflect the Lord's glory, are being transformed into his likeness with ever-increasing glory, which comes from the Lord, who is the Spirit.

- Ephesians 4:22-24 - ...put on the new self, created to be like God in true righteousness and holiness.

- Philippians 2:12-18 - ...so that you may become blameless and pure, children of God ... in which you shine like stars in the universe as you hold out the word of life--

- I P℮ter 1:13-16, L℮viticus 11:44-45, 20:7-8 - ... "Be holy, because I am holy."
- I John 2:15-17 - ...The world and its desires pass away, but the man who does the will of God lives forever.

Seeking to reflect the Lord by what I do and say

Living, well-watered

Two grapevines, growing side by side
    One well-watered,
        One water-deprived!

The well-watered vine grows vibrant and tall
    With lush green leaves from spring to fall.
With hardy branches growing in all directions
    Producing plump juicy fruit to luscious perfection
Vines well-watered, given tender loving care
    Bringing forth sweet firm fruit, that none can compare.

While the vine that grows being water-deprived
    Is straggly, barren and can barely survive.
Its branches are almost devoid of leaves
    With no new growth that one can perceive.
The sparse fruit is shriveled falling down from the vine
    Not good for anything, not even poor wine.

What a difference water has on these two growing vines
    Their care and nurturing being well defined
For without water a plant will soon fade and die
    Without life's very essence, the plant can't abide.
But with God's life-giving nutrients, sun and water
    A vine produces and produces, over and over.

We can most certainly compare to these two separate vines
    For we can be well-watered
        Or spiritually water-deprived

Would we not desire to be a well-watered vine?
    Planted in the soil of Christ, there to abide?

Nurtured by God, our Gardener, who tends with loving care
    Making us prosper and fruitfully fare.
Fed with nutrients by the food of God's living Word
    Causing us to be obedient to what we have heard.
Growing in the light of the Holy Spirit's presence
    Reflecting God's love and His very essence

For a well-watered life is vibrant and alive
    For God nurtures that life to abundantly grow and thrive.
Bringing forth fruit that lasts, touching lives every day
    Abundant spiritual fruit…God's bounty on display
But lives that refuse to follow the call that God gives
    Refusing God's guidance, choosing their way to live
Opting to go their selfish direction and not to obey
    Will reap separation and destruction on Judgment day

God's Word and Christ's love nurture our very soul
    Causing us to thrive and spiritually grow.
For without God's Word and faithful instruction
    We would slowly wither and die without any direction.
God's Spirit waters our hearts with His love and His peace
    As we trust in Him, all our striving will cease.
Would we not desire to be well-watered by the Lord?
    For joy and fruitfulness will be ours forevermore.

SCRIPTURES:

- PSALM 1 ALL – v.3 – He is like a tree planted by streams of water, which yields its fruit in season.

- ISAIAH 20:21, 61:3 – …a planting of the LORD for the display of his splendor.

- JOEL 2:28-32, ACTS. 2:17-21 – '…I will pour out my Spirit on all people,…and everyone who calls on the name of the LORD will be saved.'

- MATTHEW 7:15-23 - …by their fruit you will recognize them.
- JOHN 4:1-26 – …the gift of God –living water – v.13-14 – Indeed , the water I give him will become in him a spring of water welling up to eternal life.
- JOHN 15:1-17 – I am the true vine and my Father is the gardener. …he prunes so that it will be even more fruitful…This is to my Father's glory, that you bear much fruit, showing yourselves to be my disciples.
- GALATIANS 5:22-23 – But the fruit of the Spirit is love, joy, peace, patience, kindness, goodness, faithfulness, gentleness and self-control. Against such things there is no law.

Desiring to be well-watered by the Lord and produce fruit.

By the Wayside

The garden beckons!
Trimming, weeding, fertilizing, watering, cultivating
Maintenance
The needful and necessary!
Time, toil and tender care
OR
Ignoring!
Going and doing other things
Wandering away from a part of God's Creation
Away from a garden that can bring joy and beauty
A tragic wandering with dire results
Untrimmed, straggly bushes
Weeds tall and going to seed
Scrawny unfed bushes and plants with wilted dying flowers
Neglected untilled ground
Fruitlessness
Unsightly chaos
A garden in disarray growing wild
Everything going by the wayside!

Life beckons!
Not unlike a garden
A life filled with choices and priorities
Worldly wants and desires calling us aside
To wander away from the Sovereign One who loves us
OR
To choose daily to seek God Almighty
Doing what is needful, necessary
Maintaining a loving relationship with the Lord
OR
Ignoring Him!

With no regard to having God in your life!
A tragic wandering with dire results
A straggly faith, sporadic and sparse
Having no substance
Dotted with sin here and there
Without repentance
Unfed without the food of God's Word
Neglecting time with the Lord
Not growing
Not maturing
Fruitless in service
Unsightly, chaotic
Looking too much like the world
In disarray, going wild
With no purpose; not following God's plan
A life going by the wayside!

Oh, come back!
With a heart that yearns to be close to God!
Desiring to fellowship with Him
To be surrounded by His loving arms, within His care
A oneness! A sweet communion!
Heart to heart with your precious Savior
For there is no better place to be
Close to Him
For He is worthy of all our praise!
Come close to Christ's "wounded" side!
By His "Way" side!

Scriptures:

- Psalm 34:8-11 - Taste and see that the LORD is good;…those who seek the LORD lack no good thing.
- Psalm 42:1-2 - …my soul pants for you, O God. My soul

thirsts for God, for the living God.

- PROVERBS 4:18-27 – The path of the righteous is like the first gleam of dawn…make level paths for your feet and take only ways that are firm.
- PROVERBS 8:17 – I love those who love me, and those who seek me find me.
- ISAIAH 53 ALL - …But he was pierced for our transgressions, he was crushed for our iniquities;…and the LORD has laid on him the iniquity of us all.
- MATTHEW 10:37-39; 16:24-28; LUKE 14:27 - Then Jesus said to his disciples, "If anyone would come after me, he must deny himself and take up his cross and follow me."
- ACTS 9:2; 19:9,23; 22:4; 24:14, 22 - …followers of the Way…

Seeking to stay in God's way amidst the busyness of life

Dancing in Mid-air

God's early morning light
Revealing the dawning of a new day!
The air fresh and crisp
The dazzling sun peeking over the rooftops
In a flashing burst of energy
A mere speck against the brightening sky
Hovering in space
Hummingbirds with quickly fluttering wings
Gathering at the bird feeder
Visiting all the awakening flowers
Skirting here and there for bugs coming off the lawn
Two or three together in harmony
Dancing in mid-air!
Dodging this way and that, doing the "tango" in flight
Back and forth around the feeder
Alighting from time to time to take a drink
Piercing the feeder with their long extended beaks
Savoring the sweet nectar
Off to dance the "tango" once again, around and around
Dancing in mid-air!
Chirping with high pitched sounds
Clicking and buzzing around your ears
Proclaiming the morning
Displaying God's wondrous creation
Small and obscure, perhaps unnoticed to some
But joyous to behold
Beautiful in iridescent colors
A hummingbird delight!
Dancing in mid-air!

The start of a new beginning

Choices at the break of day
Houses and rooftops, cars and school buses
Directions to be taken
Agendas and priorities to be met
How will this day be filled?
Will it start with nourishment from God's Word?
A taste of God's Holy nectar
Refreshing, guiding and nurturing
Will we seek to gather around His Word?
To taste and see that the Lord is good
Will we delight in Him?
Choosing to feed at His table drinking in His Spirit
Deeply inhaling
Fortified for the day that awaits
Proclaiming the Gospel
Living a life that is pleasing to the Lord
Full of grace and beauty for all to see
Looking forward to life eternal
Dancing joyously around the throne
Worshipping Christ our Savior and King
Dancing in worshipful awe
Gathered together with one accord
In glory and majesty before God Himself
Like dancing in mid-air forevermore!

SCRIPTURES:

- PSALM 30 ALL - ...rejoicing comes in the morning...you turned my wailing into dancing...O LORD my God, I will give you thanks forever.

- PSALM 119:103 – How sweet are your words to my taste, sweeter than honey to my mouth.

- PSALM 149:1-4 – Let them praise his name with dancing...For the LORD takes delight in his people, he crowns the humble with salvation.

- MATTHEW 6:26 –"Look at the birds of the air; they do not sow or reap or store away in barns, and yet your heavenly Father feeds them. Are you not much more valuable than they?"
- JOHN 6:53-58 – Jesus said…"the one who feeds on me will live because of me."
- REVELATION 5:6-14 – Then I looked and heard the voice of many angels…they encircled the throne…they sang: "Worthy is the Lamb, who was slain, to receive power and wealth and wisdom and strength and honor and glory and praise!"

To God be the glory forever!

Death to the Palm

Growing vigorously, steadily encroaching
Messy and uncontrollable, needing to be removed
The time has arrived to cut it down
Death to the palm
Old dead fronds are cut off first
Green ones also, one by one
Laying topsy-turvy upon the ground
Rejected and discarded
The sprouting top crown chopped off
Leaving only the center trunk reaching for the sky
Chain saws gassed up and utilized
Slice by slice the trunk slowly but steadily shortened
Reduced bit by bit
Heavy thuds
Section by section dropping to the ground below
Bark shattering, scattering in all directions
Only the root base remaining
Enter the root grinder pulverizing the protruding stump
Nothing left as evidence of the palm's existence
Total elimination with only barren ground remaining
Death to the palm complete
But, oh the possibilities!
Clean up, neatness
A new planting
Perhaps, a crape myrtle tree with light green foliage
Crinkled, crepe-like flowers in soft pink or lavender
Blooming in summer
Adding color and beauty
A gentle reflection of God's love and grace.

Is there not a spiritual parallel to be seen?

For…oh the possibilities that lay within our lives
Only one requirement…the death of "self"!
The sin that so easily encroaches into our lives
Messy and uncontrollable needing to be removed
Dependent upon the saving grace of Christ
Through His sacrifice upon the Cross
Cutting out the old sinful life
By the power of the Holy Spirit
Undesirable habits and traits that do not reflect Christ
Idolatry and sinfulness needing to be discarded
Bit by bit
Dropping out of our lives
The shattering of the old self reducing it to nothingness
Sanctification, total elimination of that which displeases God
Death to self!
Total surrender to the Lord
Bringing forth newness of life
A desire to follow Christ
Walking obediently to His Word
Producing righteousness and beauty
Service to our Lord and King
A reflection of the One who is worthy!
To the praise of His glory!

Scriptures:

- Romans 8:1-17 - …if by the Spirit you put to death the misdeeds of the body, you will live because those who are led by the Spirit of God are sons of God.

- II Corinthians 3:18 – And we, who with unveiled faces all reflect the Lord's glory, are being transformed into his likeness with ever-increasing glory, which comes from the Lord, who is the Spirit.

- Galatians 5:16-26 - …Those who belong to Christ Jesus have crucified the sinful nature with its passions and desires…let us keep in step with the Spirit.

- EPHESIANS 4:17-5:2 – …You were taught, with regard to your former way of life, to put off your old self…to put on the new self, created to be like God in true righteousness and holiness… Be imitators of God…and live a life of love, just as Christ loved us…
- COLOSSIANS 3:1-17 – Rules for Holy Living
- I THESSALONIANS 4:3-8 – It is God's will that you should be sanctified…

Desiring to reflect Christ in everything I do and say

In God's Lane

It was a special birthday!
Celebrated at the local bowling lanes
The sound of pin-ball machines
Bowling lanes filled with the clatter of balls and pin setters
Lights glowing, music going!
The young adults enjoying themselves
Having fun, a good time together
Balls, shoes, lanes selected, everyone ready to "bowl"?
Bowling in anticipation of a high scoring game
First the stance, then the aim for the pins
The perfect delivery of the ball
The thud on the glossy waxed lane
Quickly rolling ever forward toward the pins
Aiming for a strike, happy with a spare!
Sometimes ending up with a split
Almost impossible to achieve in the second frame
Oft-times a "gutter ball", totally off the mark, achieving nothing
Try again!
Knocking down all the pins or just a few
The ball goes down the lane all the same
The final score!

Life is hardly "a game"!
God has provided "a lane" upon which we are to traverse in life.
God's lane being… following "The Cross of Christ"
For no one comes to the Father
Except by way of Christ's saving sacrifice
No matter the achievements obtained in life
Big or small the number
God has a goal in mind for each person's life
That you stay in His lane following after Him

Learning daily from His manual, the Bible
Growing, taking a stance for Him
Living a life that is pleasing to the Lord
Becoming more "Christ-like" day by day
We are to aim toward the goal, the prize
Eternal life with Him
"In Christ Jesus", our Lord!
Sometimes we are split in our vision
Our aim askew pulled in every direction
Drawn away by distractions of the world, not fully focused
Oft-times we end up in the "gutter"
Totally leaving the lane that the Father intends for our life
Caught in a groove going down the wrong path
Off the mark achieving nothing in life of eternal value
Time to "try again"!
Repent! Return to the Father in obedience!
Get back in the lane where Christ resides!
Having the vision of the Holy Spirit to guide us
Causing us to go in the right direction
To reach the mark! The goal!
Life eternal! The final score!

Scriptures:

- Exodus 15:13 – "In your unfailing love you will lead the people you have redeemed. In your strength you will guide them to your holy dwelling."

- Deuteronomy 5:32-33 – So be careful to do what the LORD your God has commanded you; do not turn aside to the right or to the left…so that you may live and prosper…

- Psalm 16:7-11 - …I have set the LORD always before me. … You have made known to me the path of life; you will fill me with joy in your presence, with eternal pleasures at your right hand.

- PROVERBS 4:20-27 - …Let your eyes look straight ahead… make level paths for your feet…do not swerve to the right or the left; keep your foot from evil.
- JOEL 2:12-14 - …Rend your heart…return to the LORD your God, for he is gracious and compassionate, slow to anger and abounding in love,…
- JOHN 14:6 – Jesus answered, "I am the way and the truth and the life. No one comes to the Father except through me."
- II CORINTHIANS 2:14-15 – But thanks be to God, who always leads us in triumphal procession in Christ and through us spreads everywhere the fragrance of the knowledge of him.
- PHILIPPIANS 3:12-14 - …I press on toward the goal to win the prize for which God has called me heavenward in Christ Jesus.

Desiring to stay in the center of God's lane

Melodious Song

I was early arriving to the church.
Parked the car in a parking space in the lot
Waited for awhile
In silence
Until an unexpected sound drifted through the still air
Faint at first; gaining strength and vibrancy
A melodious song
The sweetest of tunes
A violin's notes filling the air with wonder and delight
Whence cometh the wondrous sound?
Growing louder with every second
Enrapturing the soul; touching the senses
Capturing the heart with the lilt of the song
Coming into view a tall slender man
Violin in hand
Playing as he walked along the sidewalk
With a shaggy Afghan hound dog
Following along behind on a leash
A peculiar sight!
He played with confidence drawing the bow upon the strings
He played on, the streams of heavenly music coming forth
Calling the violin to be what it was meant to be
Imparting joy and peace along the way
The day was changed!
With his melodious song!

How might your day be changed?
By making music from your heart!
A song of praise to the Maker above
Your heart taking flight
Making a joyful noise unto the Lord!

With confidence
Drawing close to the heavenly throne of grace
Before the Mighty King!
Christ Jesus, our risen Lord!
Let your music come forth!
Giving praise and worth to God on High!
With joy and gladness
Expressing your wonder and delight
The joy of your salvation!
Becoming who you were meant to be
A child of God expressing adoration and praise!
And in the process…
Touching the lives of others around you
A witness of the great and mighty works of the Lord
Telling of your salvation
It may seem peculiar!
But, are we not to be a peculiar people?
Standing out in a world of despair
Making a difference
Always proclaiming the Word of God
Imparting love and peace to all we meet along the way
Sing forth!
The joy of the Lord is your strength and salvation!
Sing forth!
With a grateful heart!
Sing forth!
With your melodious song!

Scriptures:

- Psalm 118:24-29 – This is the day the LORD has made; let us rejoice and be glad in it.

- Psalm 150 All – Praise the LORD. Praise God in his sanctuary;… praise him with the strings and flute,…Let everything that has breath praise the LORD. Praise the LORD.

- EPHESIANS 5:19-20 – Sing and make music in your heart to the Lord, always giving thanks to God the Father for everything, in the name of our Lord Jesus Christ.
- HEBREWS 10:19-25 - ...let us draw near to God with a sincere heart in full assurance of faith,...

Lord, cause me to praise You more!

The Rut

Almost inescapable leading off into the distance
Perhaps through a green meadow
Oft-times down a dusty barren wasteland
"Ruts"
Once within them impossible to get out
No way to break free
Capturing the wheels of your vehicle
Leading where they have always led
Deep, dusty, well worn and highly traveled
Embanked on both sides
Encompassing
Boxed in
Sometimes rain soaked collecting puddles of water
Becoming muddied and mired
Impeding progress
Spinning tires and gripping tread and footwear
Bogged down in that same old rut again!
Do you feel that way sometimes?
On the same old pathway
The same rut of life
On the road of monotony and tedium
Doing the same things day after day
Boxed in with no escape
Encompassed with the same situations
The same problems seemingly without hope
Not making any progress
Stuck and held fast
Just spinning your wheels
Where is the end of this road?
How will I ever escape?
Where is God in all of this?

There is a way that pleases the Lord.
A pathway out of the never-ending ruts of life
A road that leads to eternal life forevermore
For those who trust and believe in God
He picks us up from where we are
And causes us to walk on the crest
Above the monotony and those things that hold us down
Giving us a sure footing
Providing a pathway of peace and joy
By the power of the Holy Spirit
The crest of adventure down a road less traveled
With God leading the way day by day
Following His guidance
Going in His direction
Doing what He wants us to do
The ruts of life still remain
But a road of life "in Christ" rises above and leads onward
Will you dare to follow Him?
Wherever He leads?
Will you make God your first love in life?

Scriptures:

- Psalm 37:23-24 — If the LORD delights in a man's way, he makes his steps firm; though he stumble, he will not fall, for the LORD upholds him with his hand.

- Psalm 40:1-5 — He (the LORD) lifted me out of the slimy pit, out of the mud and mire; he set my feet on a rock and gave me a firm place to stand.

- Matthew 7:13-14 - …narrow the road that leads to life, and only a few find it.

- Matthew 16:24-28 — Jesus said, "If anyone would come after me, he must deny himself and take up his cross and follow me."

- EPHESIANS 4:20-24 - ...put on the new self created to be like God in true righteousness and holiness.
- HEBREWS 10:19-25 - ...we have confidence to enter the Most Holy Place by the blood of Jesus, by a new and living way.
- REVELATION 2:1-7 - ...yet I hold this against you: You have forsaken your first love.

Seeking to ride on the crest of life with Christ

Perspectives

The pigeon's gentle coos drift upon the cool morning air
Soft, melodious and soothing
And yet to some annoying, unwelcomed messy birds
Perspective!
Raccoons, a delightful creature in God's creation
Cute with their masked faces, curious ways
And yet to some, destructive and pesky, uninvited visitors
Perspective!
The raging wind blowing mightily down the canyons
Bringing fresh warming air in its wake
And yet to some, tiresome, forcefully challenging
Blowing leaves and debris in all directions
Perspective!
God's wondrous creation all around us!
Glorious sunrises and dazzling sunsets
Growing trees and flowers
Amazing nature! God's wondrous expression of Himself!
And yet to some, bypassed, unnoticed and taken for granted
Perspective!

As on the material level, so goes it in the spiritual realm
God and who He is
Embraced and adored
Or
Ignored and abhorred
Man's perspective
His point of view
A belief system based upon
Self or based and lived upon God's Holy Word
Perspective!
For God and His Word is foolishness to the proud and arrogant

But to those who believe on His name
Trusting in God's saving grace
Following Christ Jesus as Lord and Savior
God's Word is truth proclaiming salvation!
Perspective!
Man's view of the Righteous One
The Holy God
Christ as the Savior of men's souls
Challenges and annoys
Man's self-centeredness and sinful ways
Perspective!
Oh, that we would have a clear view!
A heart that seeks God!
A life that desires to follow in Christ's footsteps
To trust Him daily and to pray unceasingly
How God desires to hold us close.
To teach us His ways
Desiring for us to rely upon His Holy Spirit
To obey Him whole-heartedly
For He has redeemed us and given us eternal life
Oh, that we would choose Him!
Daily seeking to listen and obey wherever He leads
Turning from our wicked ways
Toward His perspective!

Scriptures:

- DEUTERONOMY 6:4-8 - ...Love the LORD your God with all your heart and with all your soul and with all your strength.

- DEUTERONOMY 30:10-20 - ...For I command you today to love the LORD your God, to walk in his ways, and to keep his commands,...Now choose life...For the LORD is your life,...

- PSALM 105:1-4 - ...Glory in his holy name; let the hearts of those who seek the LORD rejoice. Look to the LORD and his strength; seek his face always.

- ISAIAH 53 ALL – v.6 – We all, like sheep, have gone astray, each of us has turned to his own way; and the LORD has laid on him the iniquity of us all.
- I CORINTHIANS 1:18-31 – For the message of the cross is foolishness to those who are perishing, but to us who are being saved it is the power of God. ...For the foolishness of God is wiser than man's wisdom,...
- I CORINTHIANS 2 ALL - ...but God has revealed it to us by his Spirit. ...words taught by the Spirit, expressing spiritual truths in spiritual words. ...But we have the mind of Christ.
- HEBREWS 12:1-3 - ...Let us fix our eyes on Jesus, the author and perfecter of our faith,

Lord, please give me Your perspective with a desire to follow and obey.

Mirror Image

Pristine crystal blue expanse
Hushed stillness
Quiet serenity and God's overwhelming peace
Cool invigorating air
Majestic snowy mountains across the mirror lake
Picture perfect
Reflecting upon the calm water an exact replica
The pristine mountains in double
Albeit reversely arranged in appearance
Details that you can almost touch
In liquid form
An exact representation of the real landscape
A mirror image!

A breathe of air
A cruising boat gliding over the still surface
A thrown pebble with circles reaching outward
Upon the stillness and calm
Ripples and distortions
Lost perfection
Quietness disrupted
Image lost!

Christ, our Lord
The exact representation of His Father in heaven
Grew in stature and wisdom and knowledge
In favor with God and men
Obedient unto death
Death on the Cross!
A true reflection of the One whom He loved

Our mirror's view
What do you see?
Whom do you reflect?
Our lives are meant to be a reflection of the Lord Jesus.
To exhibit His image
Christ-likeness
To bring forth His character
To be His light in the darkness
A representation of Him
Manifesting His character and appearance
For we have been transformed by His hand
Redeemed by His grace and love
A mirror image!

Do you like what you see in the mirror?
Is your image distorted; marred by sins effect?
Quietness and peace lost?
God's desire
"Return unto Me!"
"Be whom you were meant to be!"
A mirror image of Me!

Scriptures:

- GENESIS 1:27 – So God created man in his own image, in the image of God he created him; male and female he created them.

- PROVERBS 27:19 – As water reflects a face, so a man's heart reflects the man.

- LUKE 2:52 – And Jesus grew in wisdom and stature, and in favor with God and men.

- II CORINTHIANS 3:18 – And we, who with unveiled faces all reflect the Lord's glory, are being transformed into his likeness with ever-increasing glory, which comes from the Lord, who is the Spirit.

- HEBREWS 1:3 – The Son is the radiance of God's glory and the exact representation of his being,…
- I PETER 2:21-25 – …Christ…leaving you an example, that you should follow in his steps. …For you were like sheep going astray, but now you have returned to the Shepherd and Overseer of your souls.

Seeking to reflect Christ in what I do and say.

Orange Delight

Winter's sunshine blessing!
California's gold
A December, January gift
Juicy and ripe off the tree
Navel oranges in abundance
Beautiful and bursting with tangy sweet flavor
Luscious and dripping with juice
Clustered upon every branch
Tree limbs bending low to the ground
Ready to be picked and enjoyed
God's fruitful bounty
A year's worth of progressive growth
A long wait's reward
From sweet-smelling orange blossoms
To emerging tiny green pearls of potential fruit
Expanding and developing month by month
Slowly changing color
Ripening in the sunshine into a vibrant golden orange
A harvest of pure delight
A gift!
An expression of God's wondrous creation
Visibly seen and enjoyed
Orange delight!

Where does our delight reside?
In the earthly things or the heavenly realm?
The choices of our life
For God's gift is from above
Brought forth in His one and only Son
Christ Jesus, Immanuel, God with us!
Are we not to delight in Him?

The Savior of our soul
The gift beyond believing
The One we are to worship and adore
The One in whom we are to give thanks for His saving grace
For bringing us to Himself
There to reside forevermore!

Therefore…
We are to be the first-fruits of His creation
Made to delight in Him
Beautiful in His sight
Planted by His streams of living water
Nurtured by His powerful Word, infused by His Holy Spirit
Progressively growing and maturing
Changing into His image
To be Christ-like in our behavior in holiness and righteousness
Obeying His call to follow, serving others with a thankful heart
Delighting in Him and being a delight in turn
Month by month, year by year becoming a witness of our faith
An expression of the Lord visible for all to see
Proclaiming the Gospel of Christ
Yielding a harvest of fruitfulness in season
Giving God our worship and praise
Our gift of delight unto the Lord who reigns in majesty!

SCRIPTURES:

- PSALM 1:1-3 – He is like a tree planted by streams of water, which yields its fruit in season…

- PSALM 37:3-4, 23-24 – Delight yourself in the Lord and he will give you the desires of your heart

- MATTHEW 3:8, 10 – Produce fruit in keeping with repentance.

- JOHN 15:1-17 – You did not choose me, but I chose you and

appointed you to go and bear fruit—fruit that will last.

- II Corinthians 9:15 – Thanks be to God for his indescribable gift!
- James 1:17-18 - Every good and perfect gift is from above, coming down from the Father of the heavenly lights,…He chose to give us birth through the word of truth, that we might be a kind of first-fruits of all he created.

Desiring to be fruitful and follow the Lord

The Journey

Are you ready?
We're going on a trip.
Where are we going?
North through California through the Central Valley
It's long and spread out.
Hour after hour
A long journey
Mile upon mile
Field upon field of vegetables and fruit trees
Lots of cotton and tomatoes
Flat and endless in every direction
Arduous, tiresome and boring
Onward we go
Ever northward
Finally rising higher and higher
Scrub pines and brush appear
Bigger trees and stately pines
Blue sky with puffy white clouds
Majestic snow-covered mountains
Scenic and beautiful
Heavenly and peaceful
God's country!

We're on a journey
Life's journey
Day after day onward we go
Ever moving forward
Tiresome at times
Complicated and complex
Life's trials and heartaches
Challenging times and difficulties

Yet the journey continues
What is your destination?
Can you be sure of the outcome?
Will you get there by any road?
Or is there a specific path to take?

For our journey is with the Lord
It is by His leading
By His plan and His design
By His path
Going in His direction
Ever forward toward our final destination
Where there will be rejoicing and praise
No more sorrow and tears
Wearing His robes of righteousness
Feasting at His banquet table
Looking upon the glory of the Lord
Seeing Christ, our Lamb of God
Face to face
Wrapped in brilliance and splendor
Beyond imagining
In the presence of God
Surrounded by His glorious light
In His Holy City
Forever and ever!
God's blessing and reward to those who journey with Him
To those who follow closely after Him
Will you?
Take up your cross and follow Him?

Scriptures:

- Isaiah 61 All - ...I delight greatly in the LORD; my soul rejoices in my God. For he has clothed me with garments of salvation and arrayed me in a robe of righteousness,…

- MATTHEW 16:24-28 – "If anyone would come after me, he must deny himself and take up his cross and follow me."
- JOHN 11:25-26 -…and whoever lives and believes in me will never die. Do you believe this?
- I JOHN 5:11-12 – God has given us eternal life, and this life is in his Son.
- REVELATION 21:7 – He who overcomes will inherit all this, and I will be his God and he will be my son.
- REVELATION 21:22 – 22:5 - …the glory of God gives it light, and the Lamb is its lamp

Traveling onward!

Poppies Unfurled

They spring up in cement cracks and unusual places
Last year's seed coming to life growing profusely overnight
Grayish green foliage
Willowy, reaching for the sky
Having straight sturdy stems
Budding flowers encased in a cylindrical shell
Slowly coming forth prompted by the sun's radiant rays
God's warming sun bringing light and life
Causing growth
Poppies emerging out of their shell
Petals tightly intertwined
Springing to life
Unfurling one petal at a time
Until the flower gently opens to the light of day
Delicate, swaying in the breeze
A brilliant iridescent orange
Stunning in beauty
God's glory on display!
Unfurling, and slowly unfolding!

The wonderful grace of God
Changing one life at a time
Forever!
Being gradually sanctified and set apart to God
Conformed to the image of Christ
As we obey and follow closely after the Lord
Coming to life
Growing in love and grace
Seeking the Light of God's Word
Listening and acting in obedience
Shining forth to the world
Proclaiming the glory of the Lord
Being transformed in the inner parts

Having a change of heart
Turning in a new direction to be more and more Christ-like
Emerging into the kind of person that is pleasing to the Lord
Having holiness
Radiating righteousness
Speaking forth in all that we do and say
Being a display of God in us
Giving testimony of our faith for all to see
A witness of the riches of Christ
The power of the Holy Spirit to change a life
A vessel proclaiming the glory of God
Our awesome and mighty God!
What does God display in you?

SCRIPTURES:

- PSALM 119:129-133 - …The unfolding of your words gives light;… direct my footsteps according to your word; let no sin rule over me.

- ROMANS 8:29 – …to be conformed to the likeness of his Son,…

- ROMANS 12:1-2 - …be transformed by the renewing of your mind.

- II CORINTHIANS 3:18 – And we, who with unveiled faces all reflect the Lord's glory, are being transformed into his likeness with ever-increasing glory, which comes from the Lord, who is the Spirit.

- EPHESIANS 5:8-10 - …Live as children of light…find out what pleases the Lord.

- I TIMOTHY 1:12-17 - …so that…Christ Jesus might display his unlimited patience as an example for those who would believe on him and receive eternal life.

- II PETER 3:10-18 - …what kind of people ought you to be? You ought to live holy and godly lives,…grow in the grace and knowledge of our Lord and Savior Jesus Christ.

Being transformed into Christ's likeness, day by day

Hanging Out

The day was perfect!
A day spent together!
They came to swim and spend some time having fun.
Splashing, squirting
Swimming around and around the blue water of the pool
Keeping cool from the hot summer sun
A gentle breeze now and then
An azure sky, a cloud drifting by from time to time
We had a barbeque and shared a meal together
Sitting side by side around the table
Held hands and said "grace".
As the precocious little boy at the table said…
Hanging out!
He knows what family is all about.
After dinner, we made s'mores in the fire pit.
Creamy soft marshmallows and sweet yummy chocolate
We shared fireworks in the street for the fourth of July.
Folding chairs, all lined up along the sidewalk
Blazing sparklers aglow in the dark night sky
The finale to a perfect day! Hanging Out!

Oh, that we would "hang out" with our God!
Starting at the break of day to spend time alone with Him
One on one
For His desire is to "hang out" with us!
Oh, that we would have that same desire!
Devoting our time to prayer and meditation
Drawing close with an undivided whole heart
Being totally committed without distractions
Seeking to know the Father's will
Diving into His Word, enjoying His instruction, His presence

Feeding upon every word that proceeds from the mouth of God
Feasting upon His truth, quenching our thirst
Relying upon the Holy Spirit throughout the day
Also joining together with the family of God
In close fellowship, sharing with others
In communion around the banquet table
Focusing upon Christ, our Lord
Being thankful for the grace that has been shown to us
Daily looking for His return
When Christ will appear in the clouds
What a glorious day that will be!
Better than fireworks! A spectacular happening!
The coming day of the Lord!
When He brings all His children home to meet Him face to face
The final finale!
When we shall reside with Him forevermore!
To worship and adore Him!
To be in His presence throughout eternity
Together! Just hanging out!

SCRIPTURES:

- DEUTERONOMY 8 ALL - …man does not live on bread alone but on every word that comes from the mouth of the LORD…Be careful that you do not forget the LORD your God,…

- JOHN 14:6, 23-29 – Jesus answered, "I am the way and the truth and the life. No one comes to the Father except through me. …My Father will love him, and we will come to him and make our home with him.. … I am going away and I am coming back to you."

- I THESSALONIANS 4:13-5:11 - …we who are still alive and are left will be caught up together with them in the clouds to meet the Lord in the air. And so we will be with the Lord forever.

- HEBREWS 10:19-25 - ...let us draw near to God with a sincere heart in full assurance of faith,...Let us not give up meeting together,...but let us encourage one another—and all the more as you see the Day approaching.
- HEBREWS 12:1-3 - ...Let us fix our eyes on Jesus, the author and perfecter of our faith,...
- I JOHN 1:5-10 - ...But if we walk in the light, as he is in the light, we have fellowship with one another, and the blood of Jesus, his Son, purifies us from all sin.
- REVELATION 19:5-10 - ... "Hallelujah! For our Lord God Almighty reigns. Let us rejoice and be glad and give him glory! ... "Blessed are those who are invited to the wedding supper of the Lamb!"

Lord, help me to desire to "hang out" with You!

Wasteland

It's my fault!
I'm totally responsible!
I had good intentions.
The plants looked so perfect and beautiful at the nursery.
Plans for the garden
Plans to plant them today!
Well, maybe tomorrow!
I'll just water them.
Oops! Forgot!
A splash of water and they will come back.
Somehow the plants aren't looking as vibrant.
A little wilted
Maybe it's time to plant them.
No time! Maybe tomorrow!
I'll just water them again.
Planting day!
Hope my plants survive?
They look a little root-bound.
I'll just water them a little extra.
Not looking good!
Wilted, struggling and a little yellow on the leaves
Going into shock!
Turning brown and dried out
Watering is not the answer
Little by little they're fading away.
Gone and dead!
Wasted!
And…it's my fault!
I procrastinated.
Put off what I should have done today
Deadly consequences to my plants

They entered…the wasteland of my life!

Hasn't God provided each perfect day?
Twenty-four hours, seven days a week
Each day unto itself
Filled with opportunities
A purpose and a reason for us to be alive
What will we do with those days?
Only make plans in our minds
Never following through and actually doing something
Never making a difference
Never being a witness to God's saving grace
Never changing anyone's life around us
Procrastinating
Day after day
Only superficially watering
Never planting our lives permanently
Planting deep within the soil that God provides
Never bringing forth fruit or fragrant blossoms
Fruitfulness unto the Lord
Instead root-bound!
Stuck in a rut
Not doing anything
Little by little becoming stagnant
Complacent
Unused
Dead
In the wasteland of our lives!

What would God have you to do, today?

Scriptures:

- Deuteronomy 10:12-13, Micah 6:8 - …what does the LORD

your God ask of you but to fear the LORD your God, to walk in all his ways, to love him, to serve the LORD your God with all your heart and with all you soul, and to observe the LORD's commands and decrees that I am giving you today for your own good

- ISAIAH 32 ALL - ...See, a king will reign in righteousness....like streams of water in the desert...
- JOHN 6:1-15 - ... "Gather the pieces that are left over. Let nothing be wasted."
- II CORINTHIANS 9:6-15 - ...having all that you need, you will abound in every good work.
- GALATIANS 6:1-10 - ... Let us not become weary in doing good, for at the proper time we will reap a harvest if we do not give up.

Seeking God's direction ...so that, my life is not wasted!

— Pure Joy —

Yesterday was lovely! A gorgeous day!
The sun was shining brightly, a warm and balmy day
Suntan weather
Birds singing and flowers blooming
All is right with the world
But then…a change in the wind
The clouds quickly forming
Dark and threatening, foreboding and unwelcomed
Dense clouds covering the sky
Bringing pelting rain and chilling cold
A storm spreading across the sun
Torrential raindrops driven by the gusting wind
Dumping rain by the bucketfuls
Splashing and splattering everywhere against the pavement
And yet…watering the earth
Refreshing the air and causing plants and trees to grow strong
And finally dissipating and moving on
Beautiful billowy clouds parting exposing the radiant sun's rays
Blue skies ahead for now!
But another storm is on the way!
All according to God's wondrous plan!

What of the storm's of our lives?
Coming out of nowhere when we least expect them
Arising when all seems to be going well
Darkening our life to cause us heartache, anguish and pain
Trials and hardships
A real testing of our faith
Spreading across every part of our day
Splattering our life and even touching those around us
Welling up in us unwanted emotions, regret, suffering and tears.

What then?

Consider it pure joy, my brothers, whenever you face trials of many kinds, because you know that the testing of your faith develops perseverance. Perseverance must finish its work so that you may be mature and complete, not lacking anything.

– James 1:2-4

Excuse me! Pure joy?
Our trials are pure joy? You have to be kidding!
Often, we don't like the trials that God has placed in our life.
They are hard and difficult testing the very core of our being
They sometimes cause us to doubt
They cause us to take our eyes off of the Lord
And yet…without rain there would be no flowers
And flowers are such a blessing in our lives.
Dear Lord, teach us to receive all that you have for us
With a knowledge that You have only good in mind
For we desire to be mature "in You"
We want our life to be complete in every way, lacking nothing
Ready to meet You in the life to come.
For every trial, heartache, hard and challenging event
Whether a passing shower or a persistent downpour
They are all within Your plan for our life
Causing us to persevere
For within those trials there can be joy
Because God loves us enough
Molding us, refining us by each and every trial
Shaping us into the person that is pleasing to Him
Christ-like in every way
They cause us to totally cling to Him
For next to Him, beside His side, within His loving arms
Resides PURE JOY!

Scriptures:

- Romans 8:28 – And we know that in all things God works for the good of those who love him, who have been called according to his purpose.
- James 1:2-18 - …Blessed is the man who perseveres under trial…
- I Peter 1:3-9 -… you may have had to suffer grief in all kinds of trials. These have come so that your faith…may be proved genuine and may result in praise, glory and honor when Jesus Christ is revealed.
- I Peter 4:12-19 - …those who suffer according to God's will should commit themselves to their faithful Creator and continue to do good.

PBPGINFWMY – Please be patient, God is not finished with me yet!

Reflection

They sparkle like diamonds
Scattered profusely over the lawn
Glistening in the sunlight at the break of day
Upon every leaf turning ferns into shimmering lace
Capturing the sun's light
Reflecting prisms of cascading colors
Moisture from above
A damp refresher to plants and trees
"Dewdrops"
Disappearing in the warmth of the rising sun
God's reflective presence, the Creator of the universe
Seen also in the drifting clouds
In the pink of a glorious sunrise
Seen in a wheat field with stalks growing skyward
Sparkling golden, the heads of wheat translucent
Aglow reflecting the sun's vibrant light
Seen in the moon's lustrous rays reflecting over a still pond
Sparkling upon the water
Seen in the shadows of a tree's branches
Casting their reflection upon the ground beneath
All part of God's creation
All reflecting who He is; His might and greatness!

We also are a reflection
For we were made in the image of God
We were made to reflect Him!
We are to sparkle like diamonds in the world around us
Glistening brilliantly
Reflective of the One who saved us
Refreshing those around us with the truth, the Word of God
Being a witness!

Giving our testimony
Reflecting Christ in our life!
Living a life that is worthy before the Lord
However, we are so subtly disappearing into the world
Sadly, reflecting other things
We become complacent, non-committal
Blending in, not standing out!
Not looking like a child of the King!
Should we not reflect Christ in all that we do and say?
Being Christ-like in our behavior
He is the bright and morning star!
Beloved of the Father
The exact representation of God Almighty
Pure and holy and unblemished
Are we not to reflect Him?
Casting the Lord's shadow on everyone we meet
Reflecting His goodness
Doing what He would want us to do in obedience to His Word
Listening to and being led by His Spirit
Having spiritual fruit in our life
Love, joy, peace,
Patience, kindness, goodness
Faithfulness, gentleness and self-control
For God is above us all!
Will you reflect Him in your life today?
Ascribing to the Lord the honor and glory due His name!

SCRIPTURES:

- GENESIS 1:26-28 – So God created man in his own image, in the image of God he created him; male and female he created them.

- PSALM 91 ALL – v.1 – He who dwells in the shelter of the Most High will rest in the shadow of the Almighty.

- II Corinthians 3:18 — And we, who with unveiled faces all reflect the Lord's glory, are being transformed into his likeness with ever-increasing glory, which comes from the Lord, who is the Spirit.
- Galatians 5:16-25 — …let us keep in step with the Spirit.
- Philippians 2:12-18 - …in a crooked and depraved generation, in which you shine like stars in the universe as you hold out the word of life…
- Colossians 1:9-14 - …that you may live a life worthy of the Lord and may please him in every way: bearing fruit in every good work, growing in the knowledge of God, being strengthened with all power…
- Hebrews 1:3 — The Son is the radiance of God's glory and the exact representation of his being, sustaining all things by his powerful word.

Endeavoring to reflect the Lord in what I do and say

"jump"

Summertime – Fun in the sun
Sparkling waters clear and cool
Swimming pool time
Learning to swim
A growing child beside the pool's edge
With bright eyes open wide
Eager to swim
Yet
Fearful and afraid
Hesitant
"Jump son"
"Daddy will catch you"
"No, daddy, no!"
"I'm scared!"
"Jump son"
"My arms are open wide."
"I'll catch you."
"Trust me."
"Catch me, daddy"
"1-2-3"
"Here I come"
Caught in midair
Safe, secure
Embraced and hugged
Enjoying the cool water
Gleefully splashing basking in a father's arms!

All of life
Challenges and opportunities
A learning process
Faced eagerly

Yet with fear and trepidation
Uncertain of the outcome
"Jump son"
"Your Father will catch you."
"No, Lord, no!"
Jumping requires…
Stepping out in faith, moving forward energetically
Beginning something new
Trusting in You.
"Jump son"
"My arms are open wide."
"I'll protect you and go before you."
"Jump"
"Trust in Me"
"Here I come, Lord!"
"1-2-3"
Caught by Your loving arms
Safe, secure, able to do all things
No better place to be than directed by your Holy Spirit
Blessings in abundance with joy unending
Praises forevermore!
Basking in my Father's arms
So glad I "jumped"
To follow Thee!

SCRIPTURES:

- PROVERBS 16:3 – Commit to the LORD whatever you do, and your plans will succeed.

- PROVERBS 16:9 – In his heart a man plans his course, but the LORD determines his steps.

- PROVERBS 16:20 – Whoever gives heed to instruction prospers, and blessed is he who trusts in the LORD.

Summer Storm

Coming out of nowhere
Flashing starkly across the dark black sky
Electric bolts of lightning brilliantly crashing to the ground
Startling and spectacular, sounding the advancing storm
Thunderous
Rumbles reverberating and shaking the earth and air
Billowy clouds advancing, building upward
Threatening
The dramatic lightning and deafening thunder persist
Then the faint pitter-patter of raindrops
Splashing downward, pounding the concrete
Ever increasing with intensity
Finally the deluge pours forth out of the heavens
Beating down relentlessly
Rivulets of water running off in all directions
Droplets turning into hail for a short time
Slowly the storm passes
Everything drenched and watered
Clouds breaking into sunshine in glorious rays of color
Oh, the majesty of the clearing sky!
Declaring the departure of the summer storm!

They come out of nowhere without warning
Flashing into a Christian's walk of faith
An unwanted, petty and careless thought
A sharp cutting remark of the tongue
A selfish ungracious jester; a hint of greed and lust
Gossip rumbling out from the mouth
Sounding forth and crashing into the life of a believer!
Unbidden, making themselves known
Prompted by Satan's urgings and a sinful nature

Settling into a heart that feels justified
With an attitude of self-righteousness
A small infraction at first
Increasing, then blowing itself out of proportion
Overwhelming the heart and soul
Causing the believer to feel defeated in their walk with the Lord
Feeling worthless and unworthy
Thoughts and actions running out in rivulets
Touching those around
A hardening of the heart
In an ice cold relationship with the Lord
But…though we don't deserve it…God is faithful and forgiving!
He breaks upon the scene with outstretched arms.
Bringing conviction by the Holy Spirit
To turn a sinful life to repentance
Breaking the cycle of our rebellious leanings
Causing us to walk in newness of life
Circumcising our hearts
To follow more closely to our Lord and Savior
To be Christ-like in our thoughts and actions
Basking in the Light of His Word
Not departing from God's leading and holiness
Declaring His Sovereignty and Majesty
Resting in His Love!

SCRIPTURES:

- DEUTERONOMY 30:6 – The LORD your God will circumcise your hearts and the hearts of your descendants, so that you may love him with all your heart and with all your soul and live.

- ROMANS 1:18-32 – God's wrath against Mankind – They have become filled with every kind of wickedness, evil, greed and depravity.

- ROMANS 7:7-25 - …What a wretched man I am! Who will

rescue me from this body of death? Thanks be to God—through Jesus Christ our Lord!

- II CORINTHIANS 10:4-5 – We demolish arguments and every pretension that sets itself up against the knowledge of God, and we take captive every thought to make it obedient to Christ.
- JAMES 3:1-12 – ...out of the same mouth come praise and cursing. My brothers, this should not be.
- I PETER 1:13 – 2:12 – ...But just as he who called you is holy, so be holy in all you do; for it is written: "Be holy, because I am holy."
- II PETER 1:3-11 – His divine power has given us everything we need for life and godliness through our knowledge of him who called us by his own glory and goodness...make every effort to add to your faith...

Desiring to live holy unto the Lord!

"Busy as Bees"

The jasmine vine is blooming outside the bedroom window
White clusters of delicate star-shaped blossoms
Bright in the morning sun
Sweetly fragrant in the coolness of night
Their nectar sweet, attractive to busy bees
As you pass by, you can hear their hum
The hum of satisfaction
As the bees flit from blossom to blossom
Burrowing deeply into the flowers center
Extracting the pollen from within and continuing on to the next
Busy, busy, busy!
Only returning to the hive when the task is done
God's provision of wondrous flowers
Pollen and nectar for busy bees
All working together
Taken by the busy bees back to the hive
Transformed and made into sweet tasting honey
A miraculous transformation of their industrious labor
Sweetness of satisfaction for those who partake
Honey from the honeycomb!
The product of "busy bees"!

What is your life producing?
For a life is the sum of a man's efforts?
Right? Or maybe not!
From a worldly viewpoint…man strives to achieve
Wealth, success, security, happiness
Family, a legacy in life
But God has a different perspective.
God looks at the heart, not the achievement
Of a man…or woman…or child

- JEREMIAH 7:23-24 – Obey me, and I will be your God…
- JEREMIAH 29:11 - …For I know the plans I have for you," declares the LORD,…
- MATTHEW 16:24-28 – "If anyone would come after me, he must deny himself and take up his cross and follow me."
- JOHN 10:1-18 - …his sheep follow him because they know his voice.
- ROMANS 10:11 – "Anyone who trusts in him will never be put to shame."

Learning to "jump" in obedience to the Lord's command.

What are you producing according to God's economy?
What are you busy doing with your life?
God desires that you follow Him.
That you not merely flit from one thing to another
That your eyes are focused on Christ, your Savior
That you strive to burrow deeply into His Word
Continuing on in faith, desiring to do the Father's will
Persevering in the task set before you
Diligent and determined
For you are now transformed into who you were meant to be
A servant of the Living God!
Busy pursuing whatever the Lord leads you to do
A labor of love unto your Savior!
Because God first loved you and saved you
And in the process of serving Him with a pure heart
God will say…"Well done, good and faithful servant".
You are a sweet aroma pleasing to the Lord
You are busy about the Master's business
You are a product of the King! A child of God!
May you pursue Him seeking to do His will!
As you are "busy as bees"!

Scriptures:

- Psalm 19:7-14 - …the ordinances of the LORD are sure and altogether righteous…they are sweeter than honey, than honey from the comb.

- Psalm 119:97-104 – How sweet are your words to my taste, sweeter than honey to my mouth!

- Matthew 25:14-30 – His master replied, "Well done, good and faithful servant! You have been faithful…come and share your master's happiness!"

- I Corinthians 3:5-4:2 - …the Lord has assigned to each his task…the fire will test the quality of each man's work. Now it is required that those who have been given a trust must prove faithful.

- COLOSSIANS 3:23-24 – Whatever you do, work at it with all your heart, as working for the Lord, not for men. It is the Lord Christ you are serving.

- I THESSALONIANS 4:11-12 – Make it your ambition…to work with your hands…so that your daily life may win the respect of outsiders…

- II THESSALONIANS 3:11-13 – We hear that some among you are idle. They are not busy; they are busybodies…as for you, brothers, never tire of doing what is right.

May the Lord find me faithful in service!

THE TOUCH!

The earth in all its splendor
Touched by God's creative hand
The delicate shape of quiet snowflakes drifting downward
The sun piercing a cloudy sky in radiant glory
The vibrant colors of changing autumn leaves
The moon's glow reflecting across a still pond
Majestic mountains touched by snow covered peaks
A hummingbird in flight
Fields of grain tossed by a passing breeze
The thunderous roar of waves crashing on the shore
God's miraculous world held in the Creator's grasp
Kept by His touch!

Man's life and existence touched by God
Sustained daily, our very breath
Ordered and orchestrated by His direction
Planned before time began
Graced by His Love
Saved by His Son's sacrifice
Empowered by His Spirit
Infused by His Holy Word, God's truth for us
Kept in His care
Purposed for eternal life
In His presence, face to face
Within God's touch!

A Christmas pageant
Children in fine array ready to sing and perform
A nativity scene around a small wooden manger
That manger fashioned by a grandfather's strong rough hands
Given in love

A baby innocently lain in the manger there
Ironically
The grandson of the one who fashioned the manger years ago
That child touched by a loving grandfather
Across time and space
For that grandfather has gone to be with his Lord!
Still touching our lives today
With his loving touch!

Our touch upon a world in need
Making a difference to change the lives of others around us
Given as the Lord has given unto us
In love
Salvation's message
The touch of Christ!
Life eternal to all who believe
With care and concern
Showing comfort and bringing hospitality
Sacrificially with no thought for oneself
Generously without reservation
Touching others in gentleness
An extension of the Father's hand
Reaching out with our hands extended
The touch of His grace!

SCRIPTURES:

- GENESIS 1:27, 2:7 …God created man in his own image… formed the man from the dust of the ground.

- MATTHEW 5:14-16 – You are the light of the world

- MATTHEW 28:19-20 – …go and make disciples of all nations…

- LUKE 2:1-20 – …and she gave birth to her firstborn, a son. She wrapped him in clothes and placed him in a manger, because

there was no room for them in the inn.
- LUKE 18:15-17 – People were also bringing babies to Jesus to have him touch them…
- GALATIANS 6:9-10 – Let us not become weary in doing good…
- I JOHN 1:1 –That which was from the beginning, which we have heard, which we have looked at and our hands have touched—this we proclaim concerning the Word of life.

Seeking to touch others with the Word of life!

The Wait

We don't like to do it! Wait!
But it is self evident in the world that surrounds us.
Winter waits for spring. Spring gives rise to summer.
Summer and fall follow waiting for winter once again
The seasons, the courses they make.
The night waiting for the rise of the morning sun
The birds waiting for the break of day
Spring flowers waiting for the warmth of sunshine to return
The opening of a rose bud bursting into glory!
The slow process of each petal coming forth
Fruit trees waiting for maturity and growth
The sun's ripening affect giving forth to luscious fruit in season
The rising of a full moon
Slowly creeping upward into the night sky
Time!
A waiting! An expectation!
The wonder of God's creation!
The wait!

And so we wait!
With each new year, oh the possibilities!
A waiting of sorts with many expectations
All those New Year's resolutions!
So often, gone by the wayside in a few days
What are you waiting for? Spring? Summer?
Choose this day, whom you will serve?
This day God calls us not to wait.
God calls us to action.
Today!
Not to procrastinate, but to persevere
To grow in His grace

To mature and bring forth fruit in our lives
Daily looking to Him, dependent upon His Word
Seeking to do His will
Waiting only for His guidance and direction
Listening to the voice of the Holy Spirit!
Acting in obedience to His Word as we wait!
Waiting expectantly for Christ's return!
For this we are to wait!
Oh, come quickly Lord Jesus!
We wait in eagerness with longing to see Your blessed face
Our eyes reaching heavenward with a secure hope
The night of this world breaking forth to a new day!
The waiting over!
The wonder of the glories of heaven and eternal life

And so God waits!
For God is not willing that any should perish.
Do you know Jesus as your Savior?
What are you waiting for?

SCRIPTURES:

- JOSHUA 24:15 - …But as for me and my household, we will serve the LORD."

- PSALM 27 ALL – The LORD is my light and my salvation…one thing I ask of the LORD, this is what I seek: that I may dwell in the house of the LORD all the days of my life, to gaze upon the beauty of the LORD…wait for the LORD; be strong and take heart and wait for the LORD.

- PSALM 130:5-6 – I wait for the LORD, my soul waits, and in his word I put my hope,…

- ISAIAH 30:18 – Yet the LORD longs to be gracious to you; he rises to show you compassion. For the LORD is a God of justice. Blessed are all who wait for him!

- JOHN 16:12-15 - ...But when he, the Spirit of truth comes, he will guide you into all truth.
- ROMANS 8:18-24 - ...we ourselves, who have the firstfruits of the Spirit, groan inwardly as we wait eagerly for our adoption as sons...we wait for it patiently.
- TITUS 2:11-14 - ...live self-controlled, upright and godly lives in this present age, while we wait for the blessed hope—the glorious appearing of our great God and Savior, Jesus Christ,...
- II PETER 3 ALL - ...The Lord is not slow in keeping his promise, as some understand slowness. He is patient with you, not wanting anyone to perish, but everyone to come to repentance.

**Waiting for the blessed hope of Christ coming again!
Serving in the meantime!**

WA